CASH FLOW

Pi Luna Press

Cash Flow: A Financial Guide for Entrepreneurs

ISBN: 978-0998686080

Pi Luna Press
Santa Fe, New Mexico
www.pilunapress.com

Table of Contents

Cash Flow	1
Pricing for Profit	4
Cash Flow	62
Taxes	85

Pricing for Profit

Picking the Right Price

There are many factors involved in pricing, which include customer demand, expenses, time, etc. This chapter will teach you how to analyze different pricing strategies and make informed decisions.

What Do You Think?

How do you currently select your prices?

Meet Penny

In this book, you will be working with a sample business to help you understand the concepts and gain hands-on practice. Even if Penny's business is different from yours, the concepts will still apply. You will have an opportunity to work on your own pricing.

Art Opening

Penny is an artist and has a solo show at a gallery coming up in 6 months. To get ready, she will need to make the art, frame her pieces, and help promote the show. She wants to know how to price her work.

Breakeven Point

The first step in pricing is to know your breakeven point. The breakeven point is when the money you earn is equal to the money you spend on expenses. When you breakeven, you won't make a profit, but you also won't lose money.

Time Frame

When figuring out your breakeven point, you need to know the time period in which product sales and expenses will occur. You can choose any time period: week, month, quarter, year, etc.

What Do You Think?

What would be a good time frame for Penny's break-even analysis for her show?

Using a Spreadsheet

As we calculate Penny's breakeven point, it will be helpful to test different price points. If you do the math by hand, you'll have to recalculate each time you make a change, which is time consuming. Instead, you can use a spreadsheet to do the math for you. In this chapter, you'll learn how to set up a spreadsheet template that calculates the breakeven point.

You can use Microsoft Excel®, Google Sheets®, or Numbers for Mac®.

Parts of a Spreadsheet

A spreadsheet is a table comprised of columns, rows, and cells, which are used to organize data, make calculations, and store information.

Columns: Labeled with the letters of the alphabet and run vertically.

	A	B	C	D
1				
2				
3				

Rows: Labeled with numbers and run horizontally.

	A	B	C	D
1				
2				
3				

Cell: The intersection of a row and a column.

	A	B	C	D
1				
2				
3				

Remembering Which is Which

It is easy to mix up columns and rows. Think about rows as rowing a boat, because a boat moves side-to-side. Columns are used in architecture to support buildings, and are built vertically.

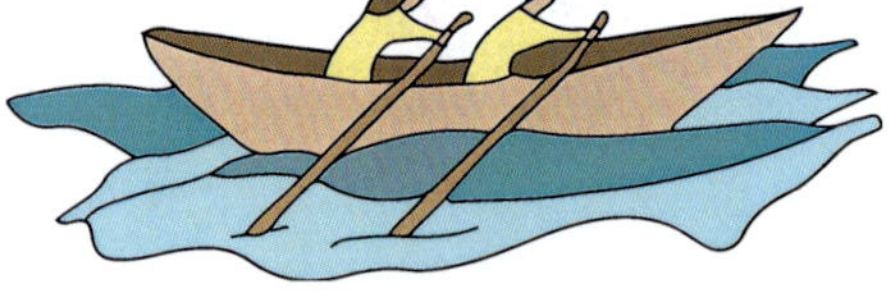

Rows

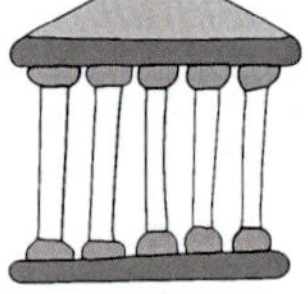

Columns

Moving Around

Being able to quickly move from one cell to the next will save you time. There are a few keyboard shortcuts worth knowing.

Move Right

To move right one cell, press the tab key on your keyboard.

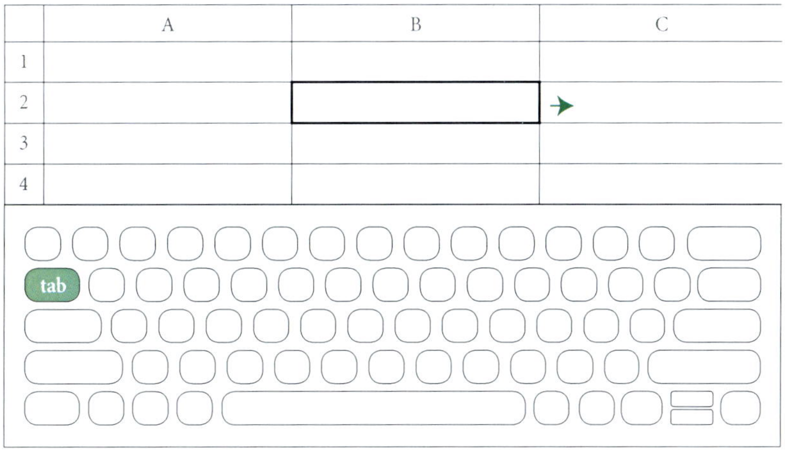

Move Left

To move left one cell, hold the shift key while pressing the tab key on your keyboard.

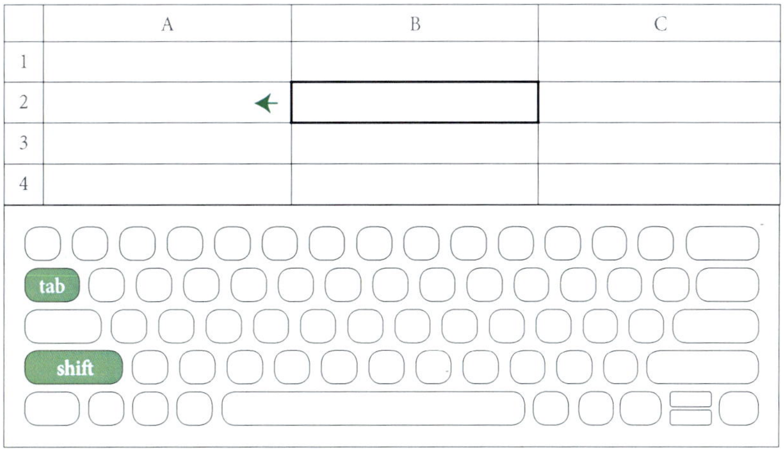

Move Down

To move down one cell, press the enter key.

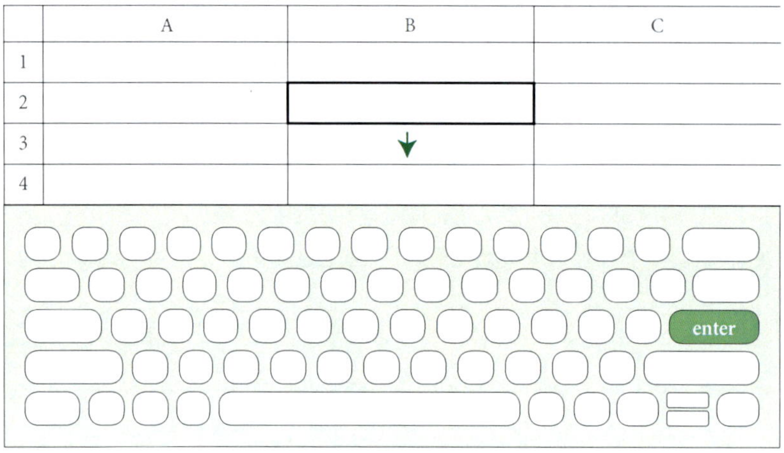

Move Up

To move up one cell, hold the shift key while pressing enter on your keyboard.

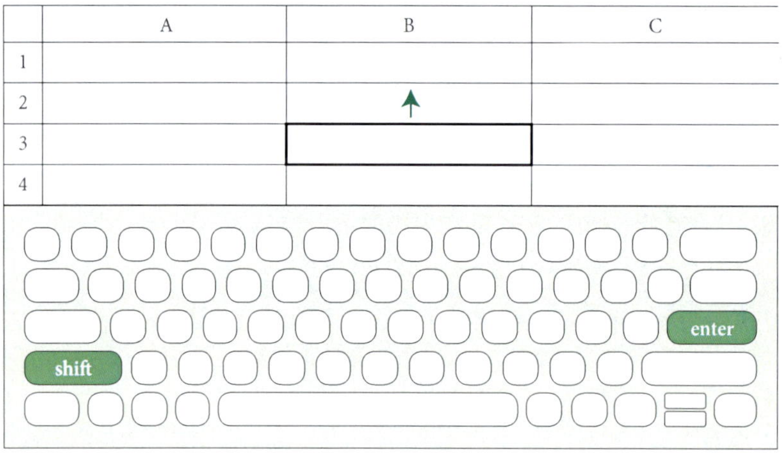

Common Keyboard Shortcuts

The following are common keyboard shortcuts.

ctrl Z	ctrl S	ctrl C	ctrl V
Undo	*Save*	*Copy*	*Paste*

Setting Up Your Spreadsheet

Step 1: Open a blank spreadsheet. You can use Microsoft Excel®, Google Sheets®, or Numbers for Mac®.

	A	B	C	D	E
1					
2					
3					

Step 2: Type the heading, "Pricing Template".

	A	B	C	D	E
1	Pricing Template				
2					
3					

Step 3: Press enter when you're done typing. The text is probably too big to fit inside the cell.

	A	B	C	D	E
1	Pricing Template				
2					
3					

Step 4: To fit the problem you can make the cell wider. Place your cursor between column letters A and B.

	A	B	C	D	E
1	Pricing Template				
2					
3					

Step 5: Click, hold, and drag to the right.

	A	→	C	D	E
1	Pricing Template				
2					
3					

Step 6: Let go of the mouse and the column width will adjust creating more room for the text.

	A	B	C	D
1	Pricing Template			
2				
3				

Retail Price

Now that your spreadsheet is setup, it's time to start filling in information about your product. The retail price is what your customers will pay for a single product.

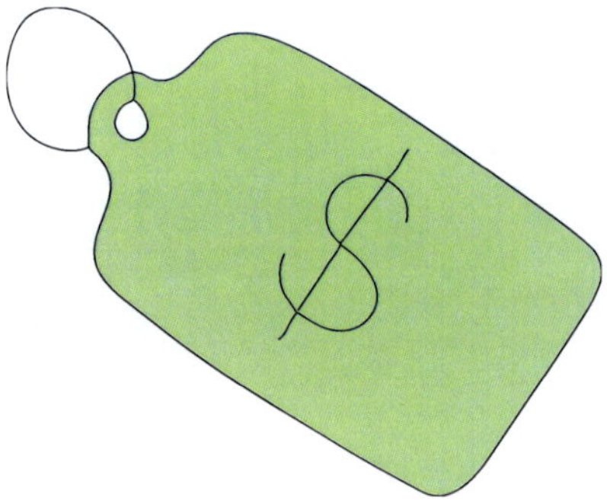

Penny is planning to charge $2000 for her paintings.

Enter the Retail Price

Step 7: Under "Pricing Template", type the heading "Retail Price".

	A	B	C	D
1	Pricing Template			
2	Retail Price			
3				

Step 8: In column B, type the retail price.

	A	B	C	D
1	Pricing Template			
2	Retail Price	2000		
3				

Wholesale Price

Since Penny is selling through a gallery, she won't receive the full selling price. The gallery will take a commission and give her the rest. The amount she will receive is called the wholesale price.

Penny's gallery is going to take a 50% commission.

Working with Percentages

When dealing with commissions, the gallery's percentage and your percentage will always add to 100%. For example, if Penny's gallery takes a 20% commission, they she will get 80%.

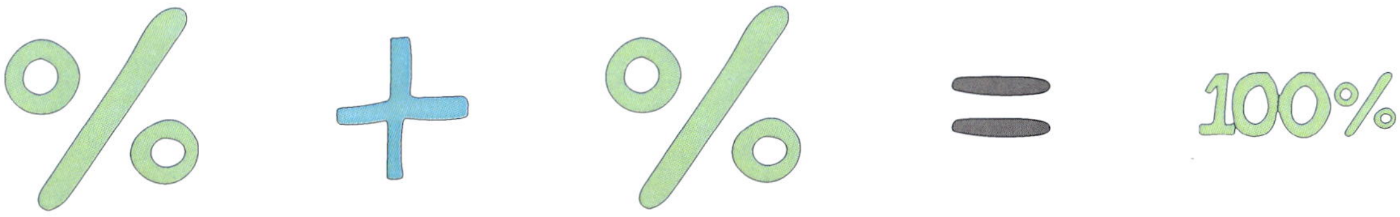

Gallery's Cut *Your Cut* *100%*

Penny's Wholesale Price

1. If Penny's gallery takes a 40% commission, what percentage does she receive?

2. If the retail price of a painting is $2000, how much will her wholesale price be?

Spreadsheets Do Math

The calculation you just made was fairly easy, but you don't want to have to recalculate every time the selling price or variable cost changes. Let the spreadsheet do the math for you.

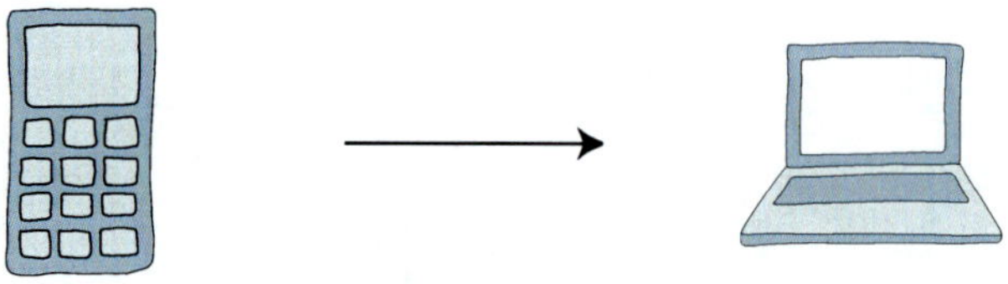

Creating Formulas

Anytime you want your spreadsheet to make a calculation, start by typing an equal sign. Then type the formula. When you're done, press enter and your spreadsheet will do the math for you.

Start with an equal sign.

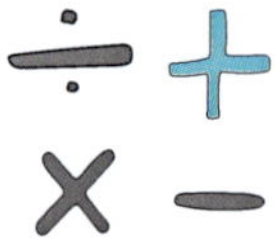

Then type a formula.

Press enter to make the calculation.

Math Symbols on Your Keyboard

In order to create formulas, it is useful to know how to find math symbols on your keyboard. Use the following keyboard shortcuts to create your formulas.

Add

Subtract

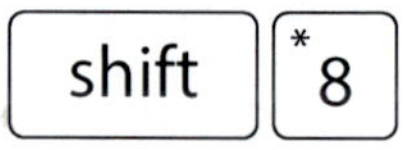

Multiply

Divide

Cell References

If you want to make calculations with numbers that are already in your spreadsheet, you don't have to retype them. Instead, you can reference those cells in your formula.

Cell Names

When you reference other cells, the cell name will show up in your formula. The cell name is the column number followed by the row number.

	A	B	C
1			
2		B2	
3			

Getting Out of a Formula

When using formulas, it's easy to make a mistake. Sometimes you need to start over, but if you click on a blank cell to get out, it just creates another cell reference, making the problem worse. Just press the escape key to get out.

Press the escape key on your keyboard to get out.

Pound Signs

If you get a series of pound signs when making a calculation, the answer is too big to fit in the cell. Just widen the cell to fix it.

	A	B	C
1	############		
2			

Calculate the Wholesale Price

Step 9: Under "Retail Price" type the heading "Wholesale Price".

	A	B	C	D
1	Pricing Template			
2	Retail Price	2000		
3	Wholesale Price			

Step 10: Click on cell B3 and type an equal sign to start a formula.

	A	B	C	D
1	Pricing Template			
2	Retail Price	2000		
3	Wholesale Price	=		

Step 11: Click on the retail price. It will become highlighted and its cell name B2 will appear in your formula.

	A	B	C	D
1	Pricing Template			
2	Retail Price	2000		
3	Wholesale Price	=B2		

STEP 12: Multiply it by 50%. (To get the multiplication symbol, press the shift and 8 keys on your keyboard.)

	A	B	C	D
1	Pricing Template			
2	Retail Price	2000		
3	Wholesale Price	=B2*50%		

STEP 13: Press enter and the wholesale price will calculate.

	A	B	C	D
1	Pricing Template			
2	Retail Price	2000		
3	Wholesale Price	1000		

VARIABLE COSTS

Once you know your pricing, you also need to factor in your costs. There are different types of costs. The variable cost is the cost of producing one product. It only includes expenses related to that particular product, so it won't include expenses like rent or utilities. Those fall under a different category.

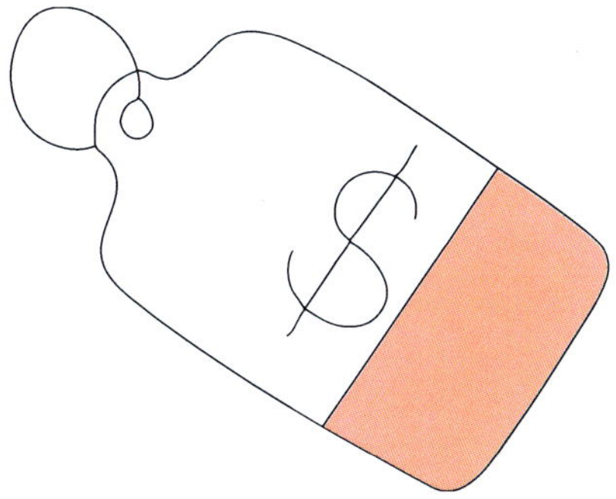

Penny's variable cost for a painting will include her supplies and labor.

Note About Service Based Businesses

If your business does not have products, but you provide services like therapy, massage, tutoring, etc, your variable costs will be your time.

Enter Variable costs

Step 14: Skip a space and type the heading "Variable costs".

	A	B	C	D
1	Pricing Template			
2	Retail Price	2000		
3	Wholesale Price	1000		
4				
5	Variable costs			

Canvas and Frame

Penny needs to buy a canvas and frame for each painting. These will be part of her variable costs.

Each canvas costs 50 and each frame costs 100.

Enter Canvas and Frame Costs

Step 15: Under "Variable costs" type the heading "Canvas".

	A	B	C	D
5	Variable costs			
6	Canvas			

Step 16: Type the cost of a single canvas.

	A	B	C	D
5	Variable costs			
6	Canvas	50		

Step 17: Type the heading "Frame".

	A	B	C	D
5	Variable costs			
6	Canvas	50		
7	Frame			

Step 18: Type the cost of a single frame.

	A	B	C	D
5	Variable costs			
6	Canvas	50		
7	Frame	100		

Paint

Some costs can be used for multiple products. For example, a tube of paint can be used to create several paintings. Penny can spread the variable cost out. To calculate the variable cost of paint, divide the cost of a tube of paint by the number of paintings it will create.

Cost of Paint *Number of Paintings*

Cost of Paint

1. If Penny buys a set of oil paints for $120 and they will last for 5 paintings, how much is her variable cost for paint?

Enter Paint Costs

Step 19: Under "Frame" type the heading "Paint".

	A	B	C	D
5	Variable costs			
6	Canvas	50		
7	Frame	100		
8	Paint			

STEP 20: Click on cell B8 and type an equal sign to start a formula.

	A	B	C	D
5	Variable costs			
6	Canvas	50		
7	Frame	100		
8	Paint	=		

STEP 21: Type the total cost of the paint, divided by the number of paintings that can be produced with the paint. (Use a dash / for division).

	A	B	C	D
5	Variable costs			
6	Canvas	50		
7	Frame	100		
8	Paint	=120/5		

STEP 22: Press enter and the unit price of paint will calculate.

	A	B	C	D
5	Variable costs			
6	Canvas	50		
7	Frame	100		
8	Paint	24		

LABOR

Penny spends many hours creating each painting. Her time is valuable and she should be compensated for her hard work. In order to factor in the cost of labor, Penny needs to pick an hourly rate for her work and then multiply it by the number of hours it takes to create a single piece.

Hours to Produce One Painting *Rate per Hour*

Penny's Labor

1. It takes Penny 15 hours to complete a single painting. If she wants to pay herself $20 per hour, how much is the cost of labor for one painting?

Enter Cost of Labor

Step 23: Under "Paint" type the heading "Labor".

	A	B	C	D
5	Variable costs			
6	Canvas	50		
7	Frame	100		
8	Paint	24		
9	Labor			

Step 24: Click on cell B9 and type an equal sign to start a formula.

	A	B	C	D
5	Variable costs			
6	Canvas	50		
7	Frame	100		
8	Paint	24		
9	Labor	=		

STEP 25: Type the number of hours times the rate per hour. Do not include the dollar sign in your formula. (Press shift and 8 on your keyboard for multiplication).

	A	B	C	D
5	Variable costs			
6	Canvas	50		
7	Frame	100		
8	Paint	24		
9	Labor	=15*20		

STEP 26: Press enter and the variable cost for labor will calculate.

	A	B	C	D
5	Variable costs			
6	Canvas	50		
7	Frame	100		
8	Paint	24		
9	Labor	300		

TOTAL VARIABLE COST

To calculate the total variable cost of a painting, you will add the canvas, frame, paint and labor.

Canvas and frame

+

Paints

+

Labor

SUM Function

Instead of adding each cell individually, you can use a shortcut. The word "sum" means addition. You can use the "sum" function to add a range of cells in your spreadsheet.

Let your spreadsheet do the addition for you.

How The "SUM" Function Works

The sum function will add the numbers in a range of selected cells. The name of the first cell and the last cell will show up in the formula.

	A	B
1		
2		
3		
4		
5	=sum(A1:A4)	

The name of the first cell and last cell in the range will show in the formula.

Calculate the Total Variable costs

Step 27: Under "Labor" type the heading "Total Variable costs".

	A	B	C	D
5	Variable costs			
6	Canvas	50		
7	Frame	100		
8	Paint	24		
9	Labor	300		
10	Total Variable costs			

Step 28: Click on cell B10. Type an equal sign followed by the word "sum" and then open a set of parentheses.

	A	B	C	D
5	Variable costs			
6	Canvas	50		
7	Frame	100		
8	Paint	24		
9	Labor	300		
10	Total Variable costs	=sum(		

Step 29: Place your cursor on the first variable cost in cell B6. Click, hold and drag to the last variable cost in B9. All of the variable costs should be highlighted. The name of the first and last cell in your selection will show up in your formula. (If you make a mistake, press escape on your keyboard to start again).

	A	B	C	D
5	Variable costs			
6	Canvas	50		
7	Frame	100		
8	Paint	24		
9	Labor	300		
10	Total Variable costs	=sum(B6:B9		

Step 30: Let go of the mouse and close the parentheses.

	A	B	C	D
5	Variable costs			
6	Canvas	50		
7	Frame	100		
8	Paint	24		
9	Labor	300		
10	Total Variable costs	=sum(B6:B9)		

Step 31: Press enter and the total variable costs will calculate.

	A	B	C	D
5	Variable costs			
6	Canvas	50		
7	Frame	100		
8	Paint	24		
9	Labor	300		
10	Total Variable costs	570		

SUM is Only for Adding

Now that you've used the sum function, it's tempting to want to use it for all calculations. But you can only use the "sum" function when you are adding a group of cells together. It won't work for subtraction, multiplication, or division.

Fixed Costs

There are other costs involved in running a business. Fixed expenses are not dependent on the number of products sold, such are rent, utilities, website, etc. Penny needs to pay for these expenses regardless or whether she sells any paintings.

Time Frame of Fixed Costs

When you calculate fixed costs, keep in mind the time frame for your breakeven analysis. Are you working with one month, six months, or a year?

Penny's Fixed Costs

1. If Penny pays $500 per month in rent for her studio, how much will she spend during a 6 month period?

Enter Fixed Costs

Step 32: Skip a space and type the heading "Fixed Costs".

	A	B	C	D
10	Total Variable costs	570		
11				
12	Fixed Costs			

Step 33: Type the fixed costs and their amounts.

	A	B	C	D
12	Fixed Costs			
13	Studio Rental	3000		
14	Utilities	330		
15	Website	300		

Step 34: Type the heading "Total Fixed Costs".

	A	B	C	D
12	Fixed Costs			
13	Studio Rental	3000		
14	Utilities	330		
15	Website	300		
16	Total Fixed Costs			

Step 35: Click on cell B16. Type an equal sign followed by the word "sum" and then open a set of parentheses.

	A	B	C	D
12	Fixed Costs			
13	Studio Rental	3000		
14	Utilities	330		
15	Website	300		
16	Total Fixed Costs	=sum(		

STEP 36: Place your cursor on the first fixed cost in B13. Click, hold and drag until you reach the last fixed cost in B15. Then close the parentheses.

	A	B	C	D
12	Fixed Costs			
13	Studio Rental	3000		
14	Utilities	330		
15	Website	300		
16	Total Fixed Costs	=sum(B13:B15)		

STEP 37: Press enter and the total fixed costs will calculate.

	A	B	C	D
12	Fixed Costs			
13	Studio Rental	3000		
14	Utilities	330		
15	Website	300		
16	Total Fixed Costs	3630		

BREAKEVEN ANALYSIS

Now that you have entered all of Penny's prices and costs into your spreadsheet, it's time to figure out her breakeven point and profit.

Contribution Margin

The first part of finding her breakeven point is to determine how much money she makes per sale. Customers will pay $2000 for a painting, the gallery will take a cut and give her $1000. Each painting costs money to create including the cost of supplies and her time. The money that is left over is her contribution margin.

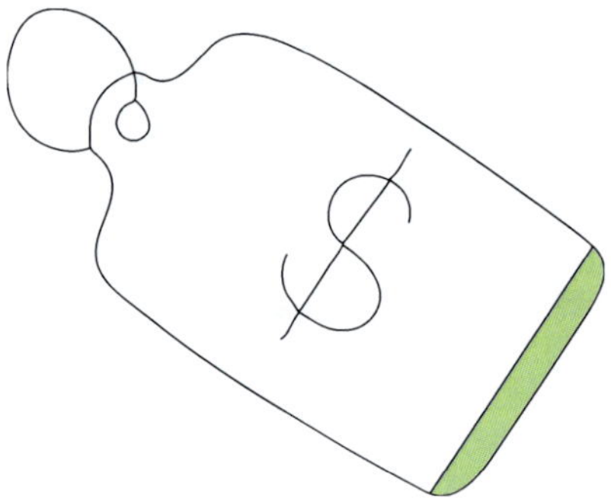

Calculating the Contribution Margin

The contribution margin is the amount of money you earn from each sale. To calculate the contribution margin, subtract the wholesale price and the variable cost.

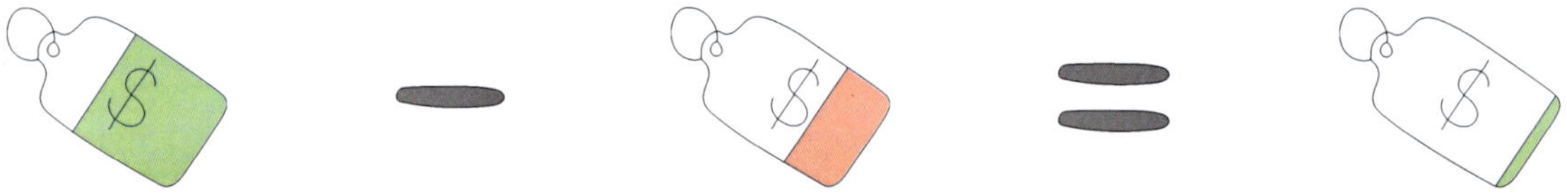

Wholesale Price | *Variable cost* | *Contribution Margin*

Calculate the Margin

1. What is Penny's contribution margin if her wholesale price is $1000 and her variable costs are $570?

Calculate the Contribution Margin

Step 38: Skip a row and type the heading "Breakeven Analysis".

	A	B	C	D
16	Total Fixed Costs	3630		
17				
18	Breakeven Analysis			

Step 39: Type the heading "Contribution Margin".

	A	B	C	D
18	Breakeven Analysis			
19	Contribution Margin			

Step 40: Click on cell B19 and type an equal sign to start a formula.

	A	B	C	D
18	Breakeven Analysis			
19	Contribution Margin	=		

STEP 41: Click on the wholesale price in B3 and subtract the total variable costs in B10.

	A	B	C	D
1	Pricing Template			
2	Retail Price	2000		
3	Wholesale Price	1000		
4				
5	Variable costs			
6	Canvas	50		
7	Frame	100		
8	Paint	24		
9	Labor	300		
10	Total Variable costs	570		
11				
12	Fixed Costs			
13	Studio Rental	3000		
14	Utilities	330		
15	Website	300		
16	Total Fixed Costs	3630		
17				
18	Breakeven Analysis			
19	Contribution Margin	=B3-B10		

STEP 42: Press enter and the contribution margin will calculate.

	A	B	C	D
18	Breakeven Analysis			
19	Contribution Margin	430		

Breakeven Point

The breakeven point is the number of products you need to sell in order to cover all your expenses. To calculate the breakeven point, divide the fixed costs by the contribution margin.

Calculate the Breakeven Point

Step 43: Under "Contribution Margin" type the heading "Breakeven Point".

	A	B	C	D
18	Breakeven Analysis			
19	Contribution Margin	430		
20	Breakeven Point			

Step 44: Click on cell B20. Type an equal sign to begin a formula.

	A	B	C	D
18	Breakeven Analysis			
19	Contribution Margin	430		
20	Breakeven Point	=		

STEP 45: Click on the total fixed costs in B16 and divide by the contribution margin in B19. (Use the dash / for division).

	A	B	C	D
12	Fixed Costs			
13	Studio Rental	3000		
14	Utilities	330		
15	Website	300		
16	Total Fixed Costs	3630		
17				
18	Breakeven Analysis			
19	Contribution Margin	430		
20	Breakeven Point	=B16/B19		

STEP 46: Press enter and the units needed to breakeven will calculate.

	A	B	C	D
18	Breakeven Analysis			
19	Contribution Margin	430		
20	Breakeven Point	8.441860465		

STEP 47: The answer is a decimal which is hard to look at. To round it to a whole number, click on the rounding icon at the top of your screen.

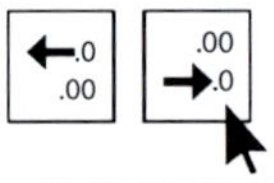

	A	B	C	D
18	Breakeven Analysis			
19	Contribution Margin	430		
20	Breakeven Point	8		

What if You Sell More?

Once you know the breakeven point, you're in a better position to predict whether you'll have a profit or loss. If you sell more units than the breakeven point, your business will make a profit. If you sell fewer, you'll have a loss.

Profit or Loss?

Let's say Penny sells 10 paintings. She will be profitable because she is selling more than her breakeven point. But how much profit will she actually earn? To calculate it, multiply the number of units sold by the contribution margin and then subtract the fixed costs.

Calculate the Profit or Loss

Step 48: Under "Breakeven Point" type the heading "Units Sold".

	A	B	C	D
18	Breakeven Analysis			
19	Contribution Margin	430		
20	Breakeven Point	8		
21	Units Sold			

Step 49: Type the number of units sold.

	A	B	C	D
18	Breakeven Analysis			
19	Contribution Margin	430		
20	Breakeven Point	8		
21	Units Sold	10		

Step 50: Type the heading "Profit or Loss".

	A	B	C	D
18	Breakeven Analysis			
19	Contribution Margin	430		
20	Breakeven Point	8		
21	Units Sold	10		
22	Profit or Loss			

Step 51: Click on cell B22. Type an equal sign to start a formula.

	A	B	C	D
18	Breakeven Analysis			
19	Contribution Margin	430		
20	Breakeven Point	8		
21	Units Sold	10		
22	Profit or Loss	=		

STEP 52: Click on the units sold in B21, multiply it by the contribution margin in B19, and subtract the fixed costs in B16.

	A	B	C	D
12	Fixed Costs			
13	Studio Rental	3000		
14	Utilities	330		
15	Website	300		
16	Total Fixed Costs	3630		
17				
18	Breakeven Analysis			
19	Contribution Margin	430		
20	Breakeven Point	8		
21	Units Sold	10		
22	Profit or Loss	=B21*B19-B16		

STEP 53: Press enter and the profit or loss will calculate.

	A	B	C	D
18	Breakeven Analysis			
19	Contribution Margin	430		
20	Breakeven Point	8		
21	Units Sold	10		
22	Profit or Loss	670		

REALISTIC PRICING

What if Penny's paintings don't sell for $2000? It's easy to choose a price that looks good, but if your product doesn't sell at that price, your guesswork won't matter. The next step is to start thinking about your audience, your market, and your competition.

Understanding Your Customers

One of the reasons Penny's work didn't sell was because she didn't understand her audience and price accordingly. When pricing your products, you need to consider who is buying your product, what they can afford, and what they are willing to pay. Art collectors, tourists, and local families will respond to pricing very differently.

Selling to Local Families

If Penny's audience is local families who want to hang custom artwork in their home, she will need to consider their budget. She may need to price her work in the $300-$500 range.

Reduced Pricing

1. Change Penny's retail price to $500 in your spreadsheet. What is her new breakeven point?

2. What is her profit or loss?

What Do You Think?

Is reducing the price a good idea for Penny? Why or why not?

Reducing Costs

When Penny reduces her prices to match her audiences' budget, she may sell more paintings, but she will be in financial trouble because her costs are more than what she is charging for her work. In order to make reducing the price profitable, she would need to reduce her costs as well.

What Do You Think?

Which of Penny's expenses do you think she could reduce?

Reduce Penny's Costs

1. Experiment with your spreadsheet and by changing Penny's costs until she is profitable. What did you change?

Changing Locations

Penny's audience might not go to galleries. Instead she could show in other locations such as coffee shops, restaurants, libraries, and churches. These locations would help her reach her target audience better and they usually take a lower commission (10%-20%). This increases her wholesale price.

By changing her location to a local coffee shop, she would receive 90% of the retail price.

Higher Wholesale Price

1. If Penny sells her work at a coffee shop, they will take 10%, which means she will get 90% of the retail price. Change your formula in the wholesale price to 90%. How profitable would Penny be?

What Do You Think?

Do you think it is a good idea for Penny to reduce her prices and her costs to match her audience? Why or why not?

Selling to Collectors

On the flip side, Penny's audience could be art collectors. In this case, pricing her art at $500 would hurt her sales. Collectors expect to pay tens of thousands of dollars on artwork (or more). If they saw a price tag that said $500, they would assume something is wrong with the piece and walk the other way.

Collectors would pay $15,000.

Raising Costs

Collectors expect a certain level of quality from the pieces they purchase. Penny might need to buy nicer frames, use higher quality materials, sell in galleries that take larger commissions, and spend longer hours creating her work. All of these elements increase her costs.

Raising Prices

1. Increase the retail price and variable costs in your spreadsheet to see what happens to Penny's breakeven point.

Building Brand Awareness

If she wants collectors to buy her work, she will also need to establish a reputation first. Collectors rarely buy work from unknown artists. She may have to gradually build a reputation before selling her work at a higher price.

What Do You Think?

If you were Penny which audience would you focus on? Which price would you choose? Why?

Multiple Products

One way Penny can find a middle path is to offer a variety of offerings. Now that you have created a spreadsheet that calculates the breakeven and profit for a single product, you can adapt it for multiple products. Let's first change the numbers in our spreadsheet back to their original values.

Return to Original Amounts

Step 54: Change the retail price back it its original amount: $2000.

	A	B	C	D
1	Pricing Template			
2	Retail Price	2000		
3	Wholesale Price	1000		

Step 55: Double-click on the wholesale price to edit the formula.

	A	B	C	D
1	Pricing Template			
2	Retail Price	2000		
3	Wholesale Price	1000		

Step 56: The formula will appear.

	A	B	C	D
1	Pricing Template			
2	Retail Price	2000		
3	Wholesale Price	=B2*90%		

STEP 57: Change the percent to 50%.

	A	B	C	D
1	Pricing Template			
2	Retail Price	2000		
3	Wholesale Price	=B2*50%		

STEP 58: Press enter and the wholesale price will update.

	A	B	C	D
1	Pricing Template			
2	Retail Price	2000		
3	Wholesale Price	1000		

STEP 59: Change the variable costs to their original amounts.

	A	B	C	D
5	Variable costs			
6	Canvas	50		
7	Frame	100		
8	Paint	24		
9	Labor	300		
10	Total Variable costs	570		

PRINTS

Penny could keep her paintings priced at $2000 and sell prints for $300. That way she can sell work that is affordable and also have higher priced items.

Add Prints to Your Spreadsheet

Step 61: At the top, type the heading "Paintings".

	A	B	C	D
1	Pricing Template	Paintings		
2	Retail Price	2000		
3	Wholesale Price	1000		

Step 62: Then in column C, type the heading "Prints".

	A	B	C	D
1	Pricing Template	Paintings	Prints	
2	Retail Price	2000		
3	Wholesale Price	1000		

Step 63: Type the retail price for the prints.

	A	B	C	D
1	Pricing Template	Paintings	Prints	
2	Retail Price	2000	300	
3	Wholesale Price	1000		

Using the Fill Handle

The wholesale price for paintings was calculated using a formula. Since the formula is already in your spreadsheet, you don't need to recreate it. Instead you can use the "fill handle" which will copy the formula into a new cell. The fill handle is located at the bottom-right corner of a cell.

The fill handle copies formulas.

Use the Fill Handle

Step 64: Click on the wholesale price for paintings in cell B3.

	A	B	C	D
1	Pricing Template	Paintings	Prints	
2	Retail Price	2000	300	
3	Wholesale Price	1000		

Step 65: Place your cursor on the fill handle on the bottom-right corner of the cell.

	A	B	C	D
1	Pricing Template	Paintings	Prints	
2	Retail Price	2000	300	
3	Wholesale Price	1000		

Step 66: Click, hold, and drag to the right to copy the formula into column C.

	A	B	C	D
1	Pricing Template	Paintings	Prints	
2	Retail Price	2000	300	
3	Wholesale Price	1000		

Step 67: Release the mouse and the formula will copy into the new cell, calculating the wholesale price for prints.

	A	B	C	D
1	Pricing Template	Paintings	Prints	
2	Retail Price	2000	300	
3	Wholesale Price	1000	150	

Average Price

Now that you have more than one price, it is difficult to determine the breakeven point with multiple prices. You will need to work with an average price. To find the average, add all of the prices together and then divide by the number of prices.

\# of prices

Penny's Average

1. What is Penny's average price if paintings sell for $2000 and prints sell for $300?

Weighted Average

The average is simple to calculate, but may not always be accurate. It assumes each type of product has the same amount of sales. In reality, some products may sell more than others.

Paintings sell 80% of the time

Prints sell 20% of the time.

Calculating the Weighted Average

To calculate the weighted average multiply the percent of sales for each product times the price for each product. Then add the results together.

percent times *the price* *percent times* *the price*

Penny's Weighted Average

1. The retail price of a painting is $2000 and paintings sell 80% of the time. The retail price of a print is $300 and they sell 20% of the time. What is the average retail price?

Enter the Average Price

Step 68: Type the heading "Average".

	A	B	C	D
1	Pricing Template	Paintings	Prints	Average
2	Retail Price	2000	300	
3	Wholesale Price	1000	150	

Step 69: Click on cell D2 and type an equal sign to start a formula.

	A	B	C	D
1	Pricing Template	Paintings	Prints	Average
2	Retail Price	2000	300	=
3	Wholesale Price	1000	150	

Step 70: Click on the retail price for paintings in B2 and multiply it by the percent that paintings sell.

	A	B	C	D
1	Pricing Template	Paintings	Prints	Average
2	Retail Price	2000	300	=B2*80%
3	Wholesale Price	1000	150	

Step 71: Type a plus symbol. Then click on the retail price of prints and multiply it by the percent that prints sell.

	A	B	C	D
1	Pricing Template	Paintings	Prints	Average
2	Retail Price	2000	300	=B2*80%+C2*20%
3	Wholesale Price	1000	150	

Step 72: Press enter and the average retail price will calculate.

	A	B	C	D
1	Pricing Template	Paintings	Prints	Average
2	Retail Price	2000	300	1660
3	Wholesale Price	1000	150	

STEP 73: Place your cursor on the fill handle and drag down.

	A	B	C	D
1	Pricing Template	Paintings	Prints	Average
2	Retail Price	2000	300	1660
3	Wholesale Price	1000	150	

STEP 74: The average wholesale price will calculate.

	A	B	C	D
1	Pricing Template	Paintings	Prints	Average
2	Retail Price	2000	300	1660
3	Wholesale Price	1000	150	830

VARIABLE COST OF PRINTS

The variable costs will be different for each product. Prints don't cost as much as paintings.

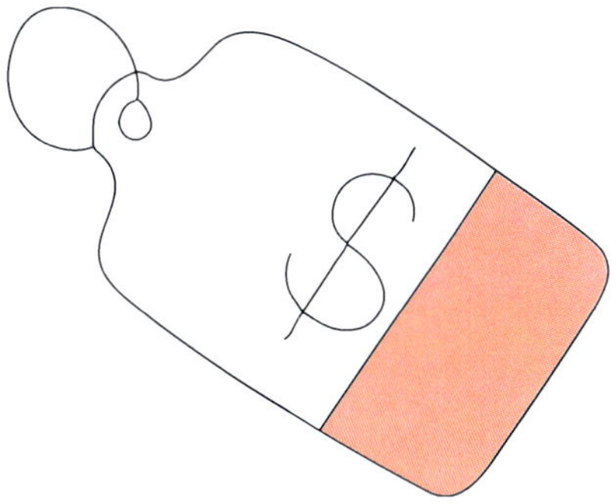

ENTER VARIABLE COSTS FOR PRINTS

STEP 75: Enter the variable costs for prints.

	A	B	C	D
5	Variable costs			
6	Canvas	50	0	
7	Frame	100	30	
8	Paint	24	0	
9	Labor	300	100	
10	Total Variable costs	570		

Step 76: To insert a new row, right-click on row number 7. Note: If you are using a Mac, press ctrl and click on the row.

	A	B	C	D
5	Variable costs			
6	Canvas	50	0	
7	Frame	100	30	
8	Paint	24	0	
9	Labor	300	100	
10	Total Variable costs	570		

Step 77: A menu will appear. Click on "Insert".

	A	B	C	D
5	Variable costs			
6	Canvas	50	0	
7	Cut	100	30	
8	Copy	24	0	
9	Insert	300	100	
10	Delete	570		

Step 78: A blank row will appear.

	A	B	C	D
5	Variable costs			
6	Canvas	50	0	
7				
8	Frame	100	30	
9	Paint	24	0	
10	Labor	300	100	
11	Total Variable costs	570		

Step 79: Click on cell A7 and type the heading "Printing".

	A	B	C	D
5	Variable costs			
6	Canvas	50	0	
7	Printing			

STEP 80: Type a zero in column B because paintings do not require printing.

	A	B	C	D
5	Variable costs			
6	Canvas	50	0	
7	Printing	0		

STEP 81: In Column C type the cost of printing.

	A	B	C	D
5	Variable costs			
6	Canvas	50	0	
7	Printing	0	75	

STEP 82: Click on the total variable costs in cell B11 and place your cursor on the fill handle on the bottom-right corner of the cell.

	A	B	C	D
10	Labor	300	100	
11	Total Variable costs	570		

STEP 83: Click, hold and drag to the right.

	A	B	C	D
10	Labor	300	100	
11	Total Variable costs	570		

STEP 84: Release the mouse and the variable costs for prints will calculate.

	A	B	C	D
5	Variable costs			
6	Canvas	50	0	
7	Printing	0	75	
8	Frame	100	30	
9	Paint	24	0	
10	Labor	300	100	
11	Total Variable costs	570	205	

Average Costs

Since you have more than one product, you'll need to find the average of the variable costs. The calculation is the same as finding the average price. Since the formula is already in your spreadsheet, you can use the fill handle to quickly do the math.

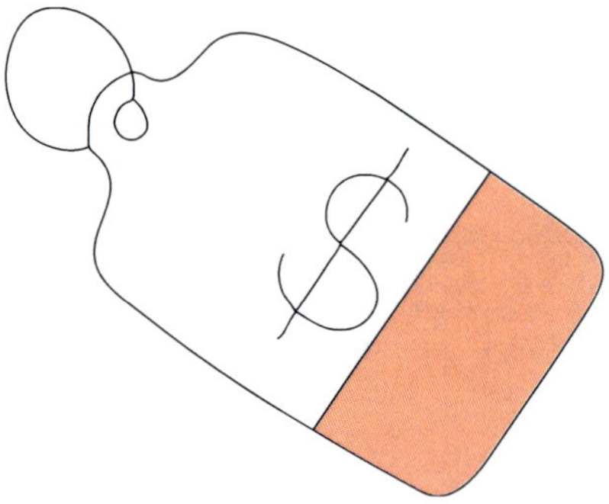

Calculate the Average Unit Price

Step 85: Click on the average wholesale price in cell D3.

	A	B	C	D
1	Pricing Template	Paintings	Prints	Average
2	Retail Price	2000	300	1660
3	Wholesale Price	1000	150	830

Step 86: Place your cursor on the fill handle and drag down.

	A	B	C	D
1	Pricing Template	Paintings	Prints	Average
2	Retail Price	2000	300	1660
3	Wholesale Price	1000	150	830
4				
5	Variable costs			
6	Canvas	50	0	
7	Printing	0	75	
8	Frame	100	30	
9	Paint	24	0	
10	Labor	300	100	
11	Total Variable costs	570	205	

STEP 87: The averages will fill in.

	A	B	C	D
1	Pricing Template	Paintings	Prints	Average
2	Retail Price	2000	300	1660
3	Wholesale Price	1000	150	830
4				0
5	Variable costs			0
6	Canvas	50	0	40
7	Printing	0	75	15
8	Frame	100	30	86
9	Paint	24	0	19.2
10	Labor	300	100	260
11	Total Variable costs	570	205	420.2

STEP 88: Delete the zeros.

	A	B	C	D
1	Pricing Template	Paintings	Prints	Average
2	Retail Price	2000	300	1660
3	Wholesale Price	1000	150	830
4				0
5	Variable costs			0
6	Canvas	50	0	40

FIXED COSTS WILL STAY THE SAME

The fixed costs won't change because they aren't related to each product.

New Contribution Margin

Currently your spreadsheet is calculating the contribution margin based on the price and costs of paintings. You will need to update the formula to include the average amounts.

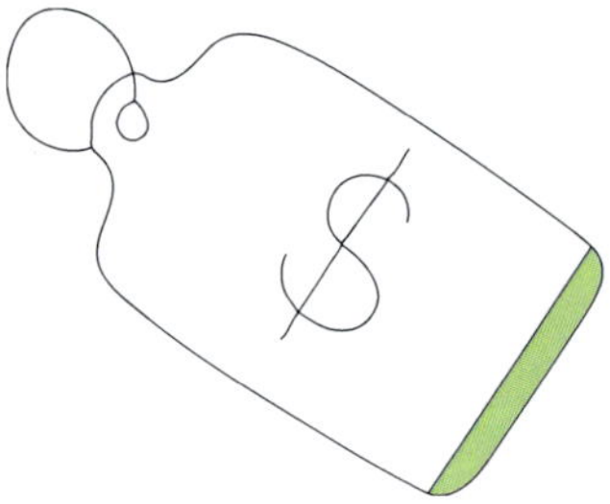

Update the Contribution Margin

Step 89: Double-click on the contribution margin in cell B20 to edit the formula.

	A	B	C	D
19	Breakeven Analysis			
20	Contribution Margin	430		

STEP 90: The current formula shows the wholesale price for paintings in B3 minus the variable costs for paintings in B11.

	A	B	C	D
1	Pricing Template	Paintings	Prints	Average
2	Retail Price	2000	300	1660
3	Wholesale Price	1000	150	830
4				
5	Variable costs			
6	Canvas	50	0	40
7	Printing	0	75	15
8	Frame	100	30	86
9	Paint	24	0	19.2
10	Labor	300	100	260
11	Total Variable costs	570	205	420.2
12				
13	Fixed Costs			
14	Studio Rental	3000		
15	Utilities	330		
16	Website	300		
17	Total Fixed Costs	3630		
18				
19	Breakeven Analysis			
20	Contribution Margin	=B3-B11		

STEP 91: Change the formula to the average wholesale price in D3 minus the average variable costs in D11.

	A	B	C	D
1	Pricing Template	Paintings	Prints	Average
2	Retail Price	2000	300	1660
3	Wholesale Price	1000	150	830
4				
5	Variable costs			
6	Canvas	50	0	40
7	Printing	0	75	15
8	Frame	100	30	86
9	Paint	24	0	19.2
10	Labor	300	100	260
11	Total Variable costs	570	205	420.2
12				
13	Fixed Costs			
14	Studio Rental	3000		
15	Utilities	330		
16	Website	300		
17	Total Fixed Costs	3630		
18				
19	Breakeven Analysis			
20	Contribution Margin	=D3-D11		

STEP 92: Press enter and the new contribution margin will calculate. The profit and loss will also update.

	A	B	C	D
19	Breakeven Analysis			
20	Contribution Margin	409.8		
21	Breakeven Point	9		
22	Units Sold	10		
23	Profit or Loss	468		

Conclusion

Now you have a spreadsheet template that you can experiment with different pricing strategies. It's helpful to have clarity about a product before selling it in real life. As your business grows, you can adapt your spreadsheet accordingly.

Pricing Summary

Vocabulary

Retail Price: The price the customer will pay for a product or service.

Wholesale Price: The price you will receive when a customer buys your product or service. It might be less than the retail price due to commissions and store markups.

Variable costs: The cost to produce a single product.

Fixed Costs: Costs that are not dependent on the number of sales.

Contribution Margin: The amount of money you earn from each sale after you subtract the variable costs.

Breakeven Point: The number of products you need to sell in order to cover all of your costs—both unit costs and fixed costs.

Units Sold: The number of products you sell.

Profit or Loss: The amount of money you earn or lose after you subtract all of your costs from your earnings.

Formulas

Contribution Margin = Wholesale Price – Variable costs

Breakeven Point = Fixed Costs ÷ Contribution Margin

Profit or Loss = Units Sold × Contribution Margin – Fixed Costs

PRICING SUMMARY

SPREADSHEET FORMULAS

	A	B	C	D
1	Pricing Template	Paintings	Prints	Average
2	Retail Price	2000	300	=B2*80%+C2*20%
3	Wholesale Price	1000	150	=B3*80%+C3*20%
4				
5	Variable costs			
6	Canvas	50	0	=B6*80%+C6*20%
7	Printing	0	75	=B7*80%+C7*20%
8	Frame	100	30	=B8*80%+C8*20%
9	Paint	24	0	=B9*80%+C9*20%
10	Labor	300	100	=B10*80%+C10*20%
11	Total Variable costs	=sum(B6:B10)	=sum(C6:C10)	=B11*80%+C11*20%
12				
13	Fixed Costs			
14	Studio Rental	3000		
15	Utilities	330		
16	Website	300		
17	Total Fixed Costs	=sum(B14:B16)		
18				
19	Breakeven Analysis			
20	Contribution Margin	=D3-D11		
21	Breakeven Point	=B17/B20		
22	Units Sold	10		
23	Profit or Loss	=B22*B20-B17		

Cash Flow

Inconsistent Income

In the last chapter you learned about product pricing and how to calculate your breakeven point. It's possible for a business to be profitable but still run out of cash. Timing matters. A cash flow statement tracks your business activities each month to help you foresee problems before they happen so you can plan ahead.

Parts of a Cash Flow Statement

In this book you will work with four basic parts of a cash flow statement.

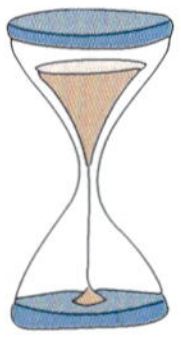

Beginning Balance
The money you have at the beginning of a month.

Cash Receipts
The money your business earns.

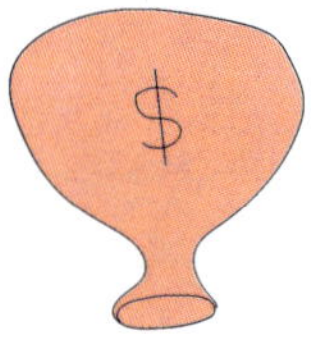

Cash Paid Out
The money your business spends.

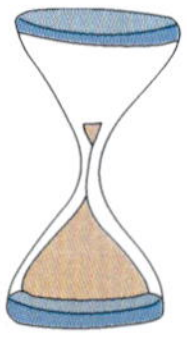

Ending Balance
The money left over at the end of the month.

Creating a New Sheet

You can create a new spreadsheet for your cash flow statement and link to the product pricing sheet you created in the last chapter.

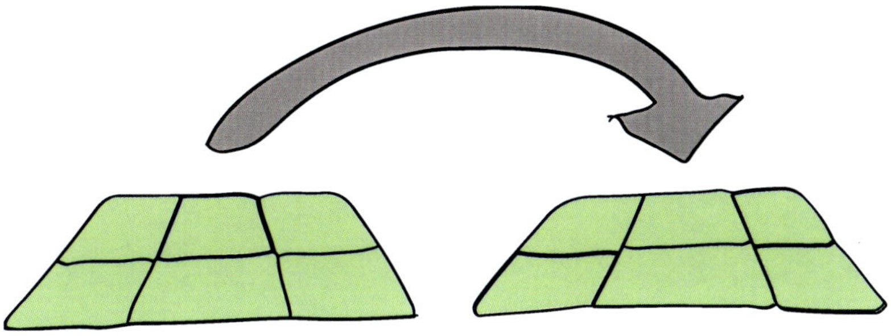

Worksheets and Workbooks

Instead of opening a new file, you can create several spreadsheets inside the same file. This makes it easier to move back and forth between them. You can also link information from one sheet to the next.

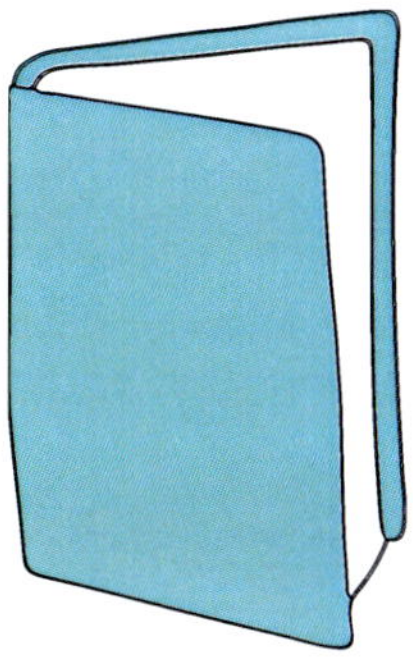

Workbook
A workbook is a single file.

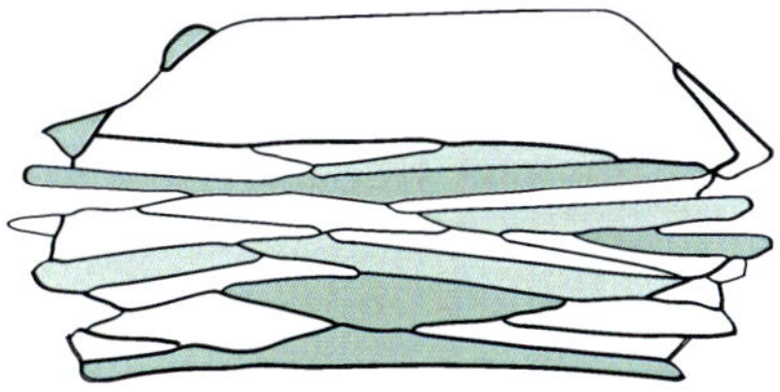

Worksheet
A worksheet is an individual spreadsheet inside a file. You can have more than one worksheet within the same workbook.

Create a New Worksheet

Step 1: Open the spreadsheet you created in the last chapter. At the bottom of the screen double-click on "Sheet 1".

	A	B	C	D
22	Units Sold	10		
23	Profit or Loss	468		
24				
25				

Sheet 1

Step 2: It will become highlighted. Rename it to "Pricing".

	A	B	C	D
22	Units Sold	10		
23	Profit or Loss	468		
24				
25				

Pricing

Step 3: Press enter and the sheet will be renamed. To create a new sheet, click on the plus symbol.

	A	B	C	D
22	Units Sold	10		
23	Profit or Loss	468		
24				
25				

Pricing +

Step 4: A blank spreadsheet will appear. Double-click on "Sheet 2".

	A	B	C	D	E
1					
2					
3					
4					
	Pricing	Sheet 2			

Step 5: Rename it to "Cash Flow". Press enter.

	A	B	C	D	E
1					
2					
3					
4					
	Pricing	Cash Flow			

Creating a Cash Flow Statement

Now that you collected information from your product pricing sheet and have created a new sheet for cash flow, it's time to start building your cash flow statement.

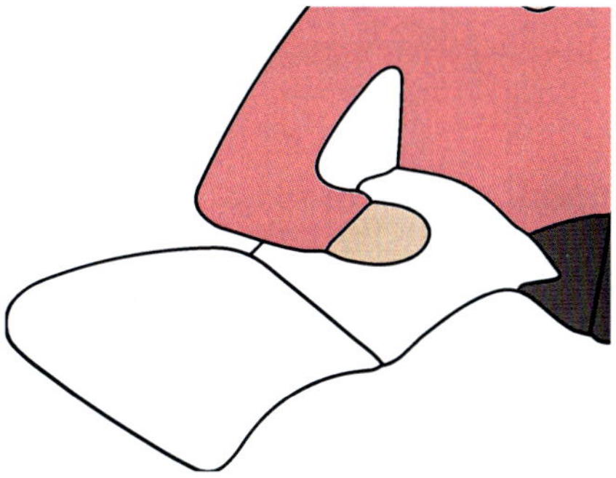

Create a Cash Flow Statement

STEP 6: Type the heading, "Cash Flow Statement".

	A	B	C	D	E
1	Cash Flow Statement				
2					
3					

STEP 7: Press enter. The text is probably too big to fit inside the cell.

	A	B	C	D	E
1	Cash Flow Statement				
2					
3					

STEP 8: To fix the problem you can make the cell wider. Place your cursor between column letters A and B.

	A	B	C	D	E
1	Cash Flow Statement				
2					
3					

STEP 9: Click, hold, and drag to the right.

	A		C	D	E
1	Cash Flow Statement				
2					
3					

STEP 10: Let go of the mouse and the column width will adjust creating more room for the text.

	A	B	C	D
1	Cash Flow Statement			
2				
3				

Step 12: Your cash flow statement should show all the months of the year. Start by typing the abbreviation for January.

	A	B	C	D
1	Cash Flow Statement	Jan		
2				

Step 13: Place your cursor on the fill handle on the bottom-right corner of the cell.

	A	B	C	D
1	Cash Flow Statement	Jan		
2				

Step 14: Drag the fill handle to the right.

	A	B	C	M
1	Cash Flow Statement	Jan		
2				

Step 15: Release the mouse and the rest of the months will fill in automatically.

	A	B	C	M
1	Cash Flow Statement	Jan	Feb	Dec
2				

Beginning Balance

The beginning balance is the amount of money you have at the beginning of the month. Penny has been saving money and will contribute $3000 of her own money to start her business. This will be her beginning balance in January.

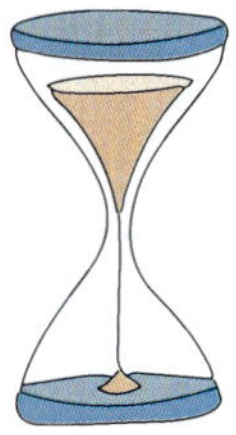

Enter Beginning Balance

Step 16: Under "Cash Flow Statement" type "Beginning Balance".

	A	B	C	D
1	Cash Flow Statement	Jan	Feb	Mar
2	Beginning Balance			

Step 17: Type the Beginning Balance for January.

	A	B	C	D
1	Cash Flow Statement	Jan	Feb	Mar
2	Beginning Balance	3000		

Cash Receipts

The next part is cash receipts, which is income received. As a business owner, your sales may fluctuate throughout the year. You can account for inconsistency in your statement.

Enter the Cash Receipts

Step 18: Skip a row and type the headings "Cash Receipts" and "Sales".

	A	B	C	D
1	Cash Flow Statement	Jan	Feb	Mar
2	Beginning Balance	3000		
3				
4	Cash Receipts			

Step 19: Type the heading "Paintings".

	A	B	C	D
4	Cash Receipts			
5	Paintings			

Step 20: Type the income from paintings for each month.

	A	B	C	D
4	Cash Receipts			
5	Paintings	0	2000	0

STEP 21: Type the heading "Prints".

	A	B	C	D
4	Cash Receipts			
5	Paintings	0	2000	0
6	Prints			

STEP 22: Type the income from prints for each month.

	A	B	C	D
4	Cash Receipts			
5	Paintings	0	2000	0
6	Prints	600	300	0

STEP 23: Type the heading "Total Cash Receipts".

	A	B	C	D
4	Cash Receipts			
5	Paintings	0	2000	0
6	Prints	600	300	0
7	Total Cash Receipts			

STEP 24: In cell B7 type an equal sign, the word "sum" and open a set of parentheses.

	A	B	C	D
4	Cash Receipts			
5	Paintings	0	2000	0
6	Prints	600	300	0
7	Total Cash Receipts	=sum(		

STEP 25: Select both of the cash receipts in cells B5 and B6. Then close the parentheses.

	A	B	C	D
4	Cash Receipts			
5	Paintings	0	2000	0
6	Prints	600	300	0
7	Total Cash Receipts	=sum(B5:B6)		

STEP 26: Press enter and the total cash receipts for January will calculate.

	A	B	C	D
4	Cash Receipts			
5	Paintings	0	2000	0
6	Prints	600	300	0
7	Total Cash Receipts	600		

STEP 27: Place your cursor on the fill handle on the bottom-right corner of the cell. Then drag across the rest of the months.

	A	B	C	D
4	Cash Receipts			
5	Paintings	0	2000	0
6	Prints	600	300	0
7	Total Cash Receipts	600		

STEP 28: The total cash receipts for each month will be calculated.

	A	B	C	D
4	Cash Receipts			
5	Paintings	0	2000	0
6	Prints	600	300	0
7	Total Cash Receipts	600	2300	0

Cash Paid Out

The cash paid out represents the expenses for a business. Expenses can fluctuate over time. Your cash flow statement is a great way to keep track of upcoming expenses, so you don't run out of cash when you need it most.

Enter the Cash Paid Out

Step 29: Skip a row and type the heading "Cash Paid Out".

	A	B	C	D
4	Cash Receipts			
5	Paintings	0	2000	0
6	Prints	600	300	0
7	Total Cash Receipts	600	2300	0
8				
9	Cash Paid Out			

Step 30: Type a list of expenses.

	A	B	C	D
9	Cash Paid Out			
10	Supplies			
11	Printing			
12	Studio			
13	Utilities			
14	Website			

STEP 31: Type the amounts for each expense under each month.

	A	B	C	D
9	Cash Paid Out			
10	Supplies	200	0	50
11	Printing	150	75	0
12	Studio	500	500	500
13	Utilities	55	55	55
14	Website	0	0	300

STEP 32: Under the last expenses, type the heading "Total Cash Paid Out".

	A	B	C	D
9	Cash Paid Out			
10	Supplies	200	0	50
11	Printing	150	75	0
12	Studio	500	500	500
13	Utilities	55	55	55
14	Website	0	0	300
15	Total Cash Paid Out			

STEP 33: Select all of the expenses and close the parentheses.

	A	B	C	D
9	Cash Paid Out			
10	Supplies	200	0	50
11	Printing	150	75	0
12	Studio	500	500	500
13	Utilities	55	55	55
14	Website	0	0	300
15	Total Cash Paid Out	=sum(B10:B14)		

STEP 34: Press enter and the total cash paid out for January will calculate.

	A	B	C	D
9	Cash Paid Out			
10	Supplies	200	0	50
11	Printing	150	75	0
12	Studio	500	500	500
13	Utilities	55	55	55
14	Website	0	0	300
15	Total Cash Paid Out	905		

STEP 35: Place your cursor on the fill handle on the bottom-right corner.

	A	B	C	D
13	Utilities	55	55	55
14	Website	0	0	300
15	Total Cash Paid Out	905		

STEP 36: Click, hold and drag the fill handle across the rest of the months.

	A	B	C	D
13	Utilities	55	55	55
14	Website	0	0	300
15	Total Cash Paid Out	905		

STEP 37: The total cash paid out for the rest of the months will be calculated.

	A	B	C	D
13	Utilities	55	55	55
14	Website	0	0	300
15	Total Cash Paid Out	905	630	905

Ending Balance

The Ending Balance represents the cash left in the business at the end of the month. Tracking it helps you make sure you don't go into the negative.

Ending Balance Formula

To calculate the Ending Balance at the end of a month, start with the Beginning Balance, add the total cash receipts, and subtract the total cash paid out.

Enter the Ending Balance

Step 38: Skip a row and type the heading "Ending Balance".

	A	B	C	D
14	Website	0	0	300
15	Total Cash Paid Out	905	630	905
16				
17	Ending Balance			

Step 39: To calculate the Ending Balance in January, type an equal sign, click on the Beginning Balance in B2, add the total cash receipts in B7 and subtract the total cash paid out in B15.

	A	B	C	D
1	Cash Flow Statement	Jan	Feb	Mar
2	Beginning Balance	3000		
3				
4	Cash Receipts			
5	Paintings	0	2000	0
6	Prints	600	300	0
7	Total Cash Receipts	600	2300	0
8				
9	Cash Paid Out			
10	Supplies	200	0	50
11	Printing	150	75	0
12	Studio	500	500	500
13	Utilities	55	55	55
14	Website	0	0	300
15	Total Cash Paid Out	905	630	905
16				
17	Ending Balance	=B2+B7-B15		

Step 40: Press enter and the Ending Balance for January will calculate.

	A	B	C	D
17	Ending Balance	2695		

February's Beginning Balance

Since the Ending Balance represents the money at the end of the month, it will carry over to the next month as the Beginning Balance.

Ending Balance in January

Beginning Balance in February

Calculate the Beginning Balance

Step 41: Click on the Beginning Balance for February and type an equal sign to start a formula.

	A	B	C	D
1	Cash Flow Statement	Jan	Feb	Mar
2	Beginning Balance	3000	=	

STEP 42: Click on the Ending Balance for January.

	A	B	C	D
1	Cash Flow Statement	Jan	Feb	Mar
2	Beginning Balance	3000	=B17	
3				
4	Cash Receipts			
5	Paintings	0	2000	0
6	Prints	600	300	0
7	Total Cash Receipts	600	2300	0
8				
9	Cash Paid Out			
10	Canvas	200	0	50
11	Printing	150	75	0
12	Studio	500	500	500
13	Utilities	55	55	55
14	Website	0	0	300
15	Total Cash Paid Out	905	630	905
16				
17	Ending Balance	2695		

STEP 43: Press enter and the Beginning Balance for February will calculate.

	A	B	C	D
1	Cash Flow Statement	Jan	Feb	Mar
2	Beginning Balance	3000	2695	

STEP 44: Place your cursor on the fill handle and drag across for the rest of the months.

	A	B	C	D
1	Cash Flow Statement	Jan	Feb	Mar
2	Beginning Balance	3000	2695	

STEP 45: Release your cursor and the beginning balance for the rest of the months will calculate. It will show zeros. That's okay, you just need to calculate ending balance for the rest of the months to fix the problem.

	A	B	C	D
1	Cash Flow Statement	Jan	Feb	Mar
2	Beginning Balance	3000	2695	-

STEP 46: Click on the ending balance in January. Place your cursor on the fill handle on the bottom-right corner of the cell. Drag across.

	A	B	C	D
17	Ending Balance	2695		

STEP 47: Let go and the ending balance as well as the beginning balance for each month will calculate.

	A	B	C	D
17	Ending Balance	2695	4365	3460

HOW IS PENNY DOING?

Based on Penny's cash flow statement, does she have any months where she is in the negative?

How much cash will she have at the end of the year?

Transferring Funds

If you are a sole proprietor, a partnership, or an LLC you can pay yourself directly from your business. This is called an "owner's draw." Your draws are considered to be part of your profit, so you can't deduct them on your tax return.

Business Account *Personal Account*

Strategies for Draws

When you pay yourself a draw, the amount and frequency of your payments is flexible. You can pay yourself when you need money. Or you can set up a system like paying yourself a percentage of your earnings or a fixed amount each month.

Sporadic Payments

Based on a Percentage

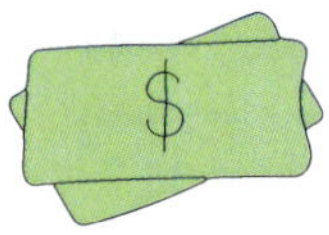

Fixed Payments

Enter the Draw in Your Cash Flow Statement

STEP 48: To insert a new row, right-click on row number 11.

	A	B	C	D
9	Cash Paid Out			
10	Supplies	200	0	50
11	Printing	150	75	0

STEP 49: A blank row will appear.

	A	B	C	D
9	Cash Paid Out			
10	Supplies	200	0	50
11				
12	Printing	150	75	0

STEP 50: Type the heading "Owner's Draw".

	A	B	C	D
9	Cash Paid Out			
10	Supplies	200	0	50
11	Owner's Draw			
12	Printing	150	75	0

STEP 51: Type an equal sign to start a formula.

	A	B	C	D
9	Cash Paid Out			
10	Supplies	200	0	50
11	Owner's Draw	=		

STEP 52: Click on the total cash receipts in cell B7 and multiply it by 30%.

	A	B	C	D
4	Cash Receipts			
5	Paintings	0	2000	0
6	Prints	600	300	0
7	Total Cash Receipts	600	2300	0
8				
9	Cash Paid Out			
10	Supplies	200	0	50
11	Owner's Draw	=B7*30%		

STEP 53: Press enter and the owner's draw in January will calculate.

	A	B	C	D
9	Cash Paid Out			
10	Supplies	200	0	50
11	Owner's Draw	180		

STEP 54: Drag the fill handle across the rest of the months.

	A	B	C	D
9	Cash Paid Out			
10	Supplies	200	0	50
11	Owner's Draw	180		

STEP 55: The owner's draw will fill in.

	A	B	C	D
9	Cash Paid Out			
10	Supplies	200	0	50
11	Owner's Draw	180	690	0

Cash Flow Summary

Vocabulary

Cash Flow Statement: A statement that tracks the income and expenses of a business over a period of time.

Beginning Balance: The amount of cash a business has at the beginning of a period.

Cash Receipts: The amount of cash a business earns during a period.

Cash Paid Out: The expenses a business pays during a period.

Ending Balance: The amount of cash a business has at the end of a period.

Formulas

Ending Balance = Beginning Balance + Total Cash Receipts - Total Cash Paid Out

Beginning Balance = Ending Balance in the previous month

Spreadsheet Template

	A	B	C	D
1	Cash Flow Statement	Jan	Feb	Mar
2	Beginning Balance	3000	=B19	=C19
3				
4	Cash Receipts			
5	Paintings	0	2000	0
6	Prints	600	300	0
7	Total Cash Receipts	=sum(B5:B6)	=sum(C5:C6)	=sum(D5:D6)
8				
9	Cash Paid Out			
10	Supplies	200	0	50
11	Owner's Draw	=B7*30%	=C7*30%	=D7*30%
12	Printing	150	75	0
13	Studio	500	500	500
14	Utilities	55	55	55
15	Website	0	0	300
16	Total Cash Paid Out	=sum(B10:B15)	=sum(C10:C15)	=sum(D10:D15)
17				
18	Ending Balance	=B2+B7-B16	=C2+C7-C16	=D2+D7-D16

Taxes

Staying Prepared

At this point, you've mapped out Penny's income and expenses in her cash flow statement and looked at her pricing. The next part is to figure out her taxes and include them in her cash flow statement so she can stay prepared.

Work with an Accountant

The material in this chapter is an introduction to taxes, so you can understand the types of taxes you need to pay and when they're due. It will help you plan ahead and stay prepared, but will not go into enough detail to teach you how to file your tax returns. Work with a CPA (certified public accountant) to calculate your exact numbers and file the paperwork.

Gross Receipts Tax

New Mexico requires businesses pay gross receipts tax, which is a percentage of their earnings. The tax rate changes based on your location.

Your Rate

Your rate depends on where your business is located. Check with your state's taxation to get an up-to-date list of tax rates.

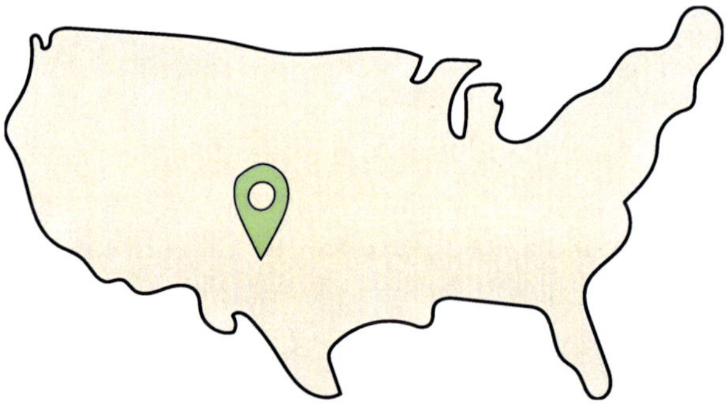

Two Methods for Gross Receipts Tax

There are a couple of ways to calculate gross receipts tax. One way is to charge your customer tax when they purchase your products or services. This is calculated the same way as sales tax. The second way is to not charge your customers tax. Instead, you "back out" the taxes from the amount of money they pay you. The result is that you end up earning less money than the selling price.

Option 1
Charge the customer.

Option 2
Back out the tax from the sale price.

Let's Review Percentages

Since calculating taxes involves percentages, let's do a quick review of working with percentages. The word percent means "out of a hundred".

Percentages and Money

One way to think about percentages is to look at money, because one dollar has 100 cents.

One Dollar *100 Pennies*

Percent of a Dollar

Each penny represents 1% of a dollar. So 5% percent of a dollar would be 5 pennies.

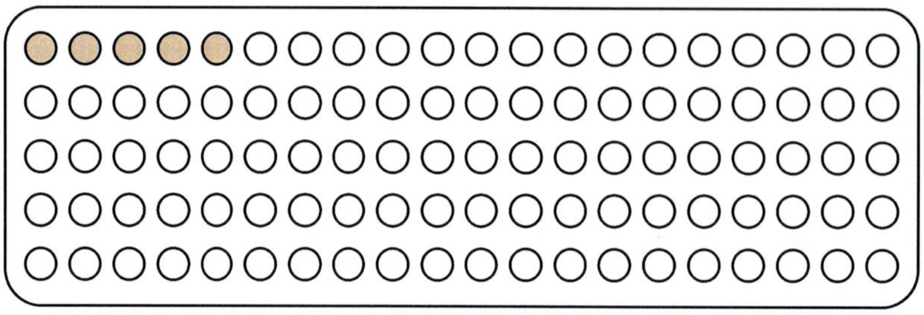

5% = 5 Pennies

Multiple Dollars

Now that you know what 5% of one dollar is, you can find 5% of other amounts. For example, 5% of two dollars would be 10 pennies.

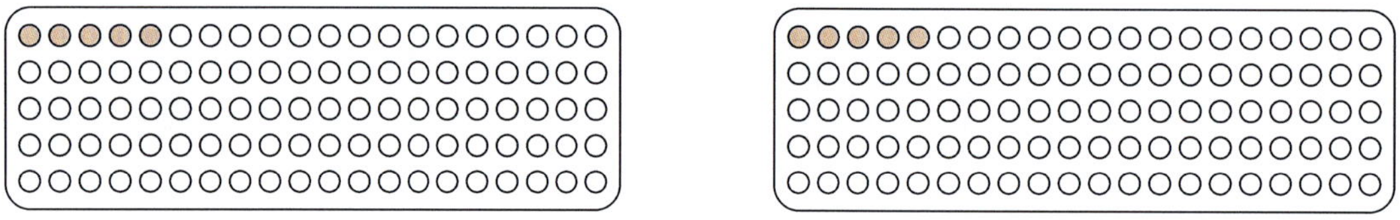

Your Turn

1. What is 5% of three dollars?

Percentages and Decimals

Every percentage has a decimal equivalent. When you looked at 5% of a dollar, you got 5 pennies. If you wrote that as money, it would look like \$0.05—that's the decimal equivalent.

$$5\% = 0.05$$

Converting Percentages

When you want to do a calculation with a percentage, convert it to its decimal equivalent first. You do this by dropping the percent symbol and dividing by 100.

$$5\% = 5 \div 100$$

Penny's Rate

1. The tax rate in Penny's location is 8.5%. What is the decimal equivalent of her rate?

Charging the Customer

Most states require sales tax, which is a percentage of the selling price that is paid by the customer. It is collected by the businesses and then paid to the state.

Calculating Sales Tax

Each city has a different tax rate. To calculate sales tax, multiply the tax rate by the selling price. Note: Make sure to convert the rate into its decimal equivalent before multiplying.

5%	×	PRICE	=	TAX
Tax Rate		*Selling Price*		*Sales Tax*

Penny's Sales Tax

1. If one of Penny's prints sells for $300 and the sales tax rate is 8.5%, how much tax will she charge?

Total Amount Paid

The total amount paid is what the customer will pay. It includes the selling price and sales tax.

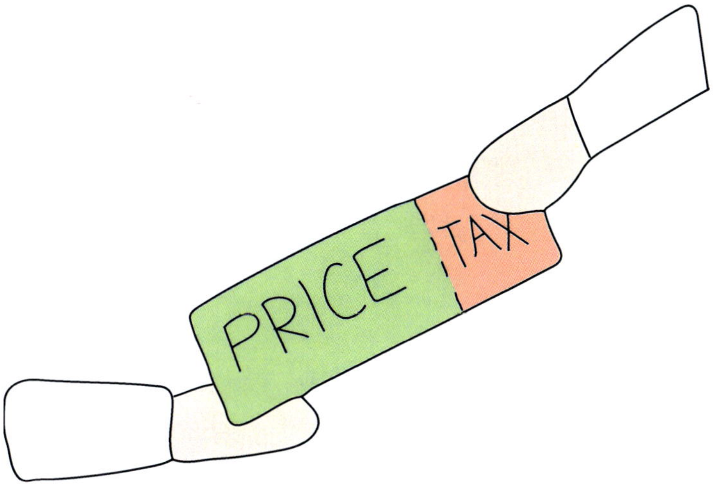

Calculating Total Amount Paid

To calculate the total amount paid, add the tax to the selling price.

Selling Price | *Sales Tax* | *Total Amount Paid*

Penny's Total Amount Paid

1. Penny's print costs $300 and the tax rate is 8.5%. How much would she charge a customer?

Shortcut to Calculating the Total Amount Paid

You just learned how to calculate the total amount paid in two steps, but there is a shortcut that lets you do it in one step. Learning the shortcut also will help you understand gross receipts tax, which comes up later in the chapter.

Looking at Percentages

Let's look at the formula you just learned in terms of percentages. The customer is charged 100% of the selling price plus a percentage of the selling price in tax to get the total amount paid.

100%	+	5%	=	100% 5%
100% of the Selling Price		*5% of the Selling Price*		*Total Amount Paid*

Simplifying the Formula

The formula can be simplified by adding the percentages together (100% + 5% = 105%). Let's call this the total rate.

105%	×	PRICE	=	PRICE TAX
Total Rate		*Selling Price*		*Total Amount Paid*

Penny's Total Rate

1. Penny's tax rate is 8.5%. What is her total rate?

Backing Out Taxes

When you back out the taxes, you split the selling price into two parts. The first part you get to keep. The second part you must pay to the state as gross receipts taxes.

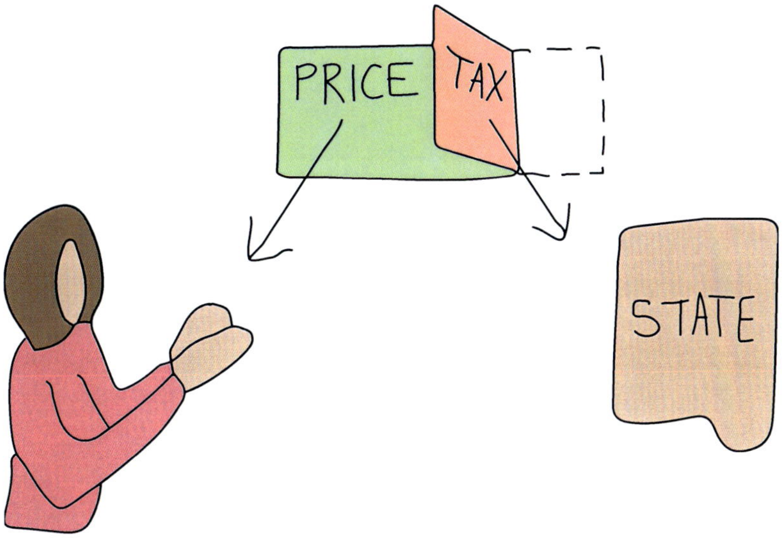

Price Before Taxes

The part that you get to keep is the price before taxes. It is less than the selling price of the product or service.

Review the Sales Tax Formula

When you learned how to calculate sales tax, you used the formula below. You'll use a similar formula for backing out tax.

Total Rate — *Selling Price* — *Total Amount Paid*

Backing Out the Tax

When you charge customers tax, you multiply the selling price by the total rate. When you back out the tax, you do the opposite: you divide the selling price by the total rate. This will give you the price before taxes.

Selling Price — *Total Rate* — *Price Before Taxes*

Penny's Price Before Tax

1. If Penny decides to back out the tax, how much of each print sale will she get to keep? Each print costs $300 and the tax rate is 8.5%.

Which Method?

Which method do you think is best: charging the customer tax or backing it out? Why?

Estimated Taxes

When you are an employee, a portion of every paycheck will be withheld to prevent you from owing a large sum of money all at once. When tax season comes around, you will have already paid most or all of your taxes. As a business owner, you don't have the same luxury. This chapter will give you an introduction to the types of taxes you will pay, when to pay them, and how to calculate them.

Estimated Payments

In order to prevent you from owing a large sum of money during tax season, the IRS requires estimated quarterly payments (4 times per year). The following are the due dates for each payment:

April 18

June 15

Sept 15

Jan 16 of the following year

Ways to Calculate Estimated Taxes

When you own a business, your income and expenses will fluctuate making it hard to predict your taxes. There are a couple of ways to calculate your estimated income taxes.

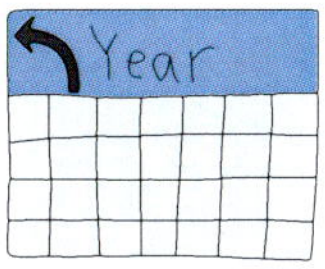

Option 1:
You can calculate your estimated payments based on last year's tax return.

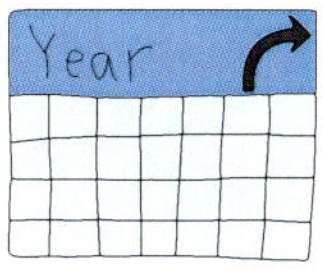

Option 2:
You can predict the amount of taxes you will owe in the upcoming year and base your payments on that amount.

Option 1: Based on Last Year's Return

The first option is to base your estimated taxes off last year's tax return. Take the amount of taxes you paid last year and then divide by 4. That will be your estimated payment each quarter.

Last Year's Taxes ÷ *4 Quarters* = *Estimated Payment*

Penny's Estimated Taxes

1. If Penny owed $3,000.00 last year, how much will her quarterly estimated payments be?

Wrong Amount

If you base your estimated tax payments off last year's taxes, you run the risk of paying too little or too much if your business performs differently from last year. The good news is that if you pay based on the previous year, you won't be charged penalties.

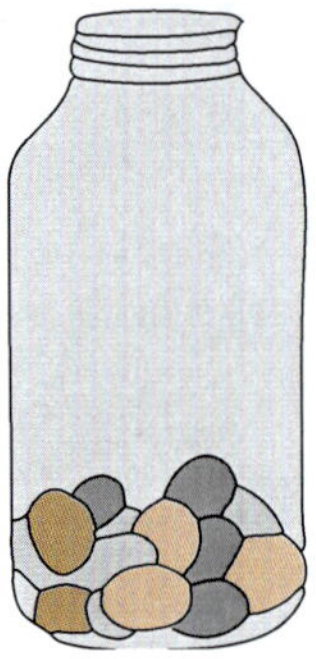

Under Paid

If you didn't pay enough to cover this year's taxes, you'll have to pay more when you file your tax return to cover the difference. You won't be charged penalties.

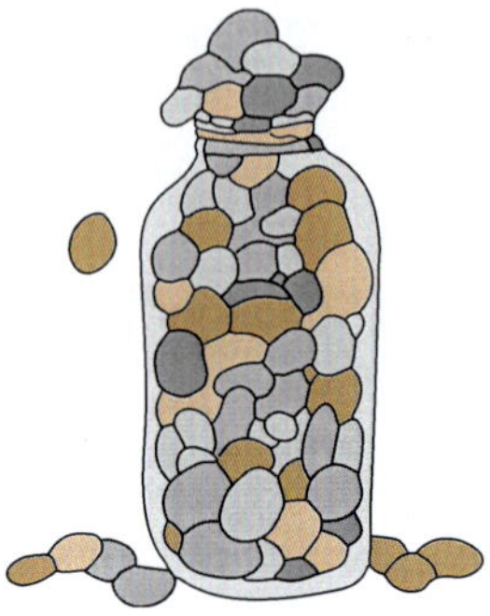

Over Paid

If you pay too much, you can choose to be reimbursed or to credit the extra amount towards the next year's taxes.

Option 2: Predict the Upcoming Year

Instead of paying taxes based on last year, you can predict the upcoming year. Depending on your business, this could help your payment be more accurate. The only downside is that if you predict incorrectly, you may be charged penalties.

Net Income

Your estimated taxes are based on your net income rather than your gross income. That means you can subtract all of your business expenses first.

Gross Income *Business Expenses* *Net Income*

Income Statement

Thankfully, you've already created Penny's cash flow statement. You can use that to make an income statement which will show the total income and expenses for the year.

Income Statement	
Gross Income	$
Expense 1	$
Expense 2	$
Expense 3	$
Total Expenses	$
Net Income	$

Home Office Expenses

If you work from home, you can deduct a percentage of your living expenses such as rent/ mortgage, insurance, utilities, Internet, etc.

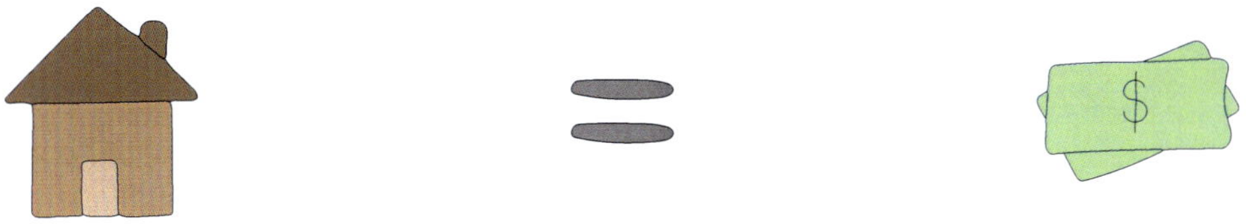

Total Square Feet

The first step to calculate your home office expenses is to find the total area of your home. You do this by multiplying the length times the width. If your home has more than one story, measure the area of each floor separately and then add them together.

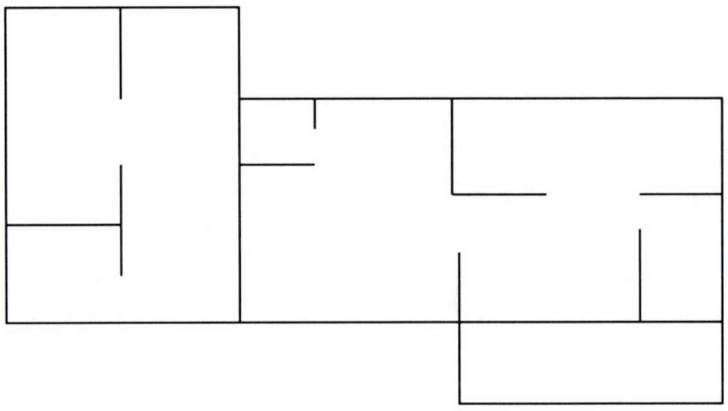

Calculating Square Feet

If the floor plan of your house is not a perfect rectangle, you can split it into several smaller rectangles and calculate the square feet for each rectangle. Then add them together to get the total area.

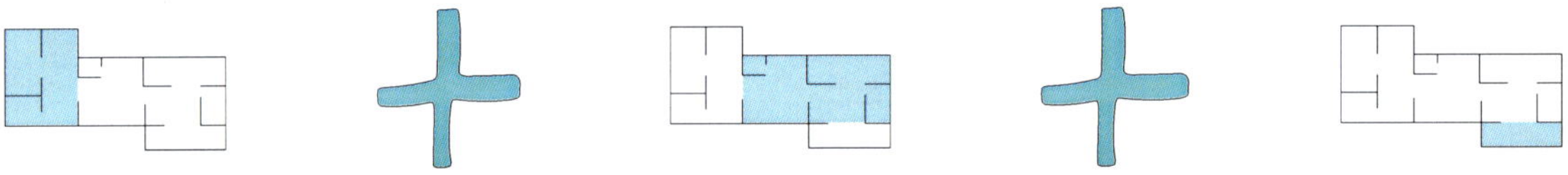

First Section *Second Section* *Third Section*

Office Square Feet

The next step is the calculate the area of your office. This space must be used solely for businesses.

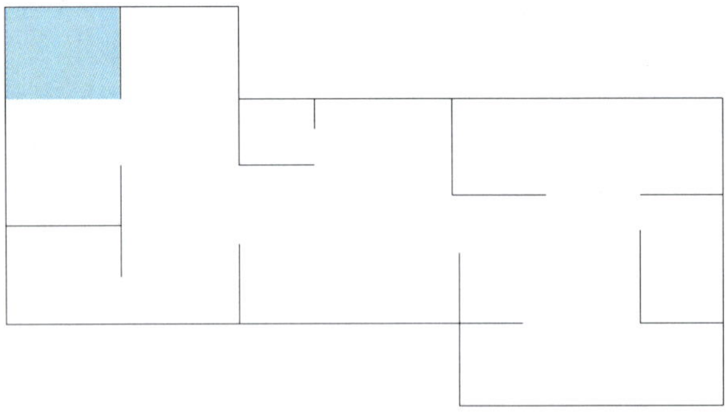

Calculate Home Office Deduction

Once you know the total area of your home and the area of your office, you can calculate your home office deduction. To do this you divide the area of the office space by the area of the total home and then multiply the result by multiplying your living expenses (rent/mortgage, insurance, utilities, internet, etc.).

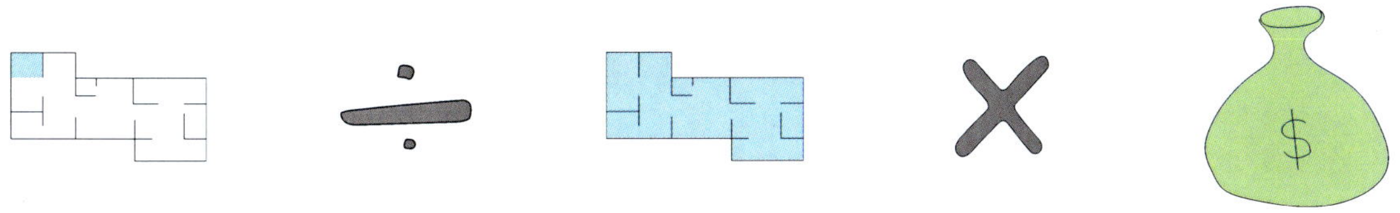

Area of Office ÷ *Total Area of Home* × *Living Expenses*

Penny's Home Office Deduction

1. Penny pays $975 for rent each month. She pays $75 for utilities per month, $24 for renter's insurance per month, and $85 for internet access per month. What are her total living expenses for the year?

2. Her condo is 1500 square feet and her home office is 375 square feet. How much can she deduct for you home office?

External Office

If you decide to work in a separate office space, you can deduct your rent, utilities for the office, and internet for the office. You can not deduct your personal living expenses.

Deducting Car Expenses

There are two ways to deduct car expenses as a business owner. You can deduct expenses based on your miles or based on your car expenses (gas, oil, insurance, car payments, etc.).

Option 1:
Deduct Miles

Option 2:
Deduct Car Expenses

Option 1: Deduct Miles

Since most people use their car for both business and personal expenses, you can deduct the miles you use for your business. The rate per mile changes each year. Check with the IRS website www.irs.gov to find the rate in your current year. In this chapter, we'll use the rate in 2017: \$0.535 per mile.

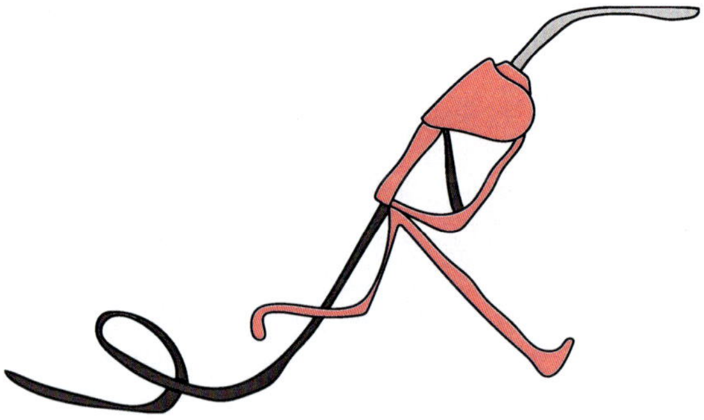

You can deduct \$0.535 per mile.

Mileage and Your Office Location

If you decide to use mileage, the rules are different if you have a home office or an external office.

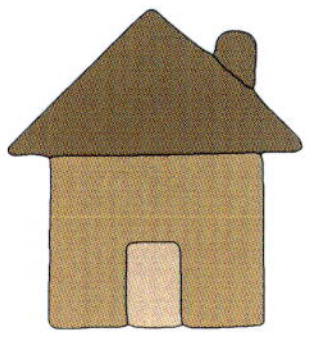

Home Office

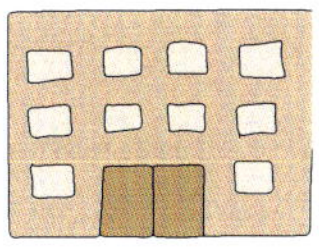

External Office

Mileage with a Home Office

If you have a home office, all of your business related miles are deductible. You will need to keep a log of your travel in order to qualify.

Mileage Log

The IRS requires you to keep track of your miles. If you get audited, you will be asked to provide documentation about the miles you deducted. The following table is an example of a mileage log. You can keep track of your miles on paper or there are several mobile apps that track the miles for you.

Date	Starting Location	Ending Location	Purpose	Beginning Mileage	Ending Mileage
5/15/17	Home	Client's House	Coaching Session	134712	134714
5/15/17	Client's House	Office Store	Print Brochures	134714	134719
5/15/17	Office Store	Home	Travel Home	134719	134725

Penny's Mileage

1. How many miles did Penny drive on May 15th shown in the previous mileage log?

2. If the IRS allows her to deduct $0.535 per mile, how much money can she deduct on that day? Round to the nearest cent.

3. If she drives that many miles on average everyday (365 days) for a year, how much money will she be able to deduct?

Mileage with an External Office

When you rent or use an office space outside of your home, only part of your miles will be deductible.

Between Your Home and Office

When you have an external office, the miles you travel between your home and your office are not deductible.

Between Your Home and Other Business Locations

When you have an external office, the miles you drive between your home and work locations other than your office (meeting a client, doing consulting work, giving a presentation, etc.) are deductible.

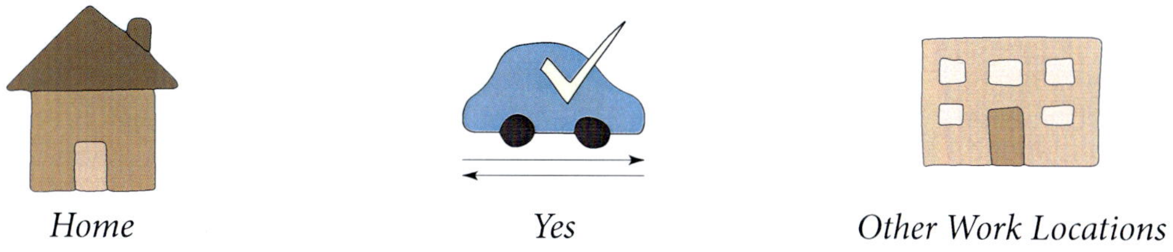

Between Your Home and Business Errands

When you have an external office, the miles you travel between your home and business related errands (going to the bank, checking your mail, printing materials, etc.) are not deductible.

Between Your Office and Other Work Locations

When you have an external office, the miles you travel between your office and other work locations (meeting a client, doing consulting work, giving a presentation, etc.) are deductible.

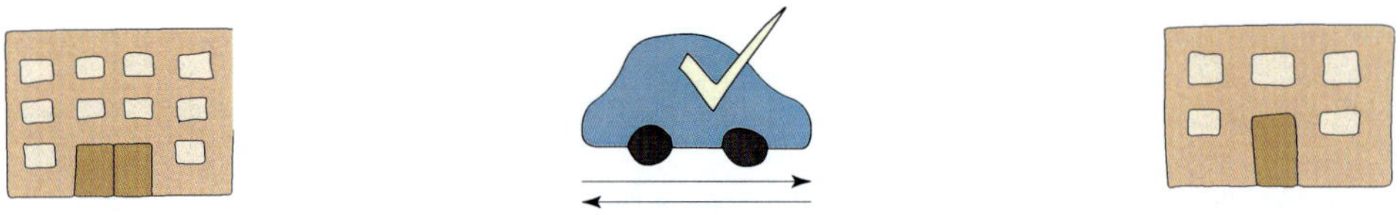

Office *Yes* *Other Business Locations*

Between Your Office and Business Errands

When you have an external office, the miles you drive between your office and business errands (going to the bank, checking your mail, printing materials, etc.) are deductible.

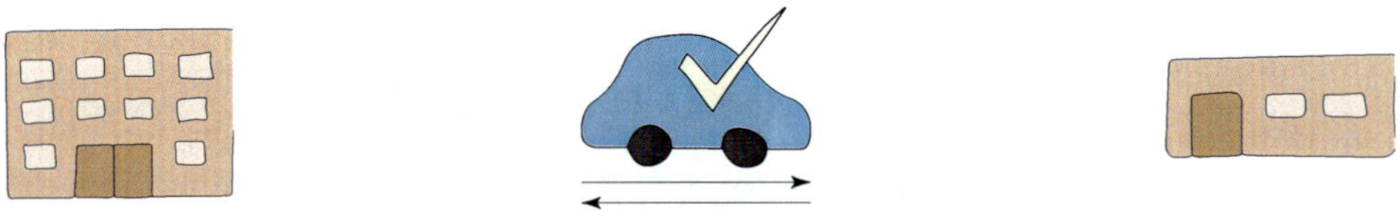

Office *Yes* *Business Errands*

Penny's Miles

The following log shows Penny's miles on May 15th. Since she has an external office,only some of those miles will be deductible.

Date	Starting Location	Ending Location	Purpose	Beginning Mileage	Ending Mileage
5/15/17	Home	Office	Commute to Work	134712	134719
5/15/17	Office	Client's House	Coaching Session	134719	134722
5/15/17	Client's House	Office Store	Print Brochures	134722	134725
5/15/17	Office Store	Office	Back to Office	134725	134731
5/15/17	Office	Home	Commute Home	134731	134737

Penny's Miles

1. Based on the mileage log in the previous paragraph, how many total miles will Penny travel on May 15th?

2. How many of those miles are deductible?

What Do You Think?

1. If you were Penny, would you use a home office or rent office space? Why or why not?

Option 2: Deducting Car Expenses

Instead of using miles, you can deduct your actual car expenses: gas, oil changes, maintenance, insurance, and car/lease payments, etc.

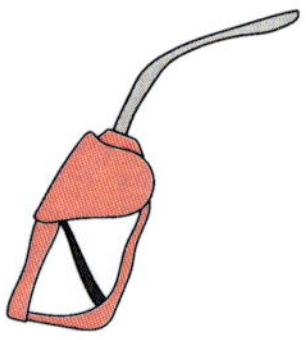

Gas

Oil Changes

Maintenance

Insurance

Depreciation

If you bought the car you are using for your business, you won't deduct your car payments. Instead you will use what's called depreciation. You car will last for several years, so the IRS wants you to spread the cost of your car out between those years.

Spreading the Cost Over Time

There are several ways to calculate depreciation, but the most common way is called the "Straight-Line Method". When you use this method, you deduct the same amount for your car each year.

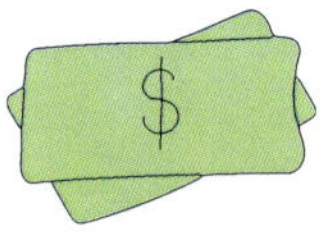

Year 1

Year 2

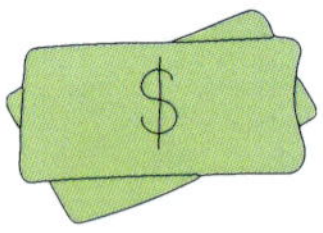

Year 3

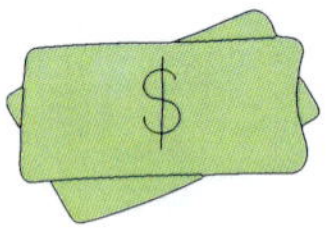

Year 4

Year 5

Useful Life

In order to calculate depreciation, you will need to know the useful life of the car, which is the number of years it is expected to last.

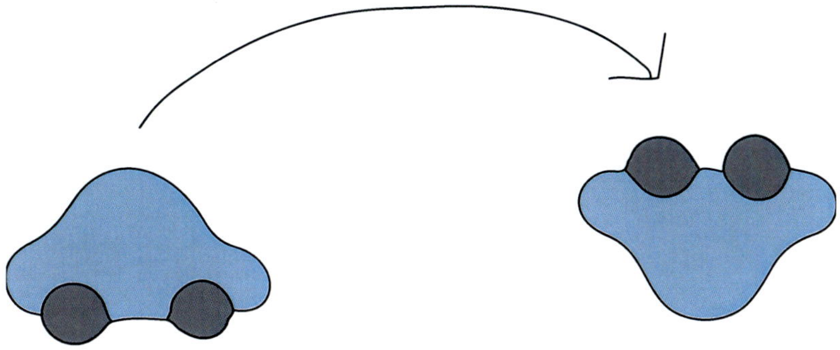

Residual Value

You will also need to know the residual value, which is the value of the car at the end of its useful life.

Calculating Depreciation

To calculate the depreciation (the amount you will deduct each year), you subtract the original value minus the residual value and then divide it by the useful life in years.

Original Value of the Car — *Residual Value* ÷ *Useful Life in Years*

MACRS

It can be hard to predict the useful life and residual value of a car. Instead of guessing, the IRS has a list of standards in MACRS (Modified Accelerated Cost Recovery System). You can work with an accountant to calculate the exact depreciation for your car.

Penny's Depreciation

1. Penny bought a new car for $30,000.00 that is expected to last 18 years, at which point it will be worth $5,000.00. How much depreciation can she deduct each year over the course of those 18 years?

2. Penny has a car loan which will last for years? Her monthly payment is $559.29 per month. How much will she spend on her car payments in the first year?

What Do You Think?

1. Based on your answers to the previous exercise, is the depreciation enough to cover Penny's car payments?
2. In which year will depreciation start paying off for Penny?
3. Do you think depreciation is fair? Why or why not?

Leases

An alternative to buying is car is to get a lease. When you lease a car you will have a monthly payment for a set period of time. During that time you can drive the car. Once the lease is up, you will return the car to the dealer. Since you do not own the car, you do not have to use depreciation. Instead you can simply deduct your lease payments.

What Do You Think?

1. If you were Penny would you buy a car or lease a car? Why or why not?

Calculating Your Deduction

Since most business owners use their car for both personal and business purposes, you will need to calculate a percentage of business use. To do this, you will still keep a mileage log as shown earlier in this section. (The home office versus external office rules still apply). Divide your business miles by the total miles and then multiply the answer by your total car expenses.

Business Miles ÷ *Total Miles* × *Total Car Expenses*

Penny's Deduction

1. Penny has $1,388.89 in depreciation from your car. She also pays on average $24.00 per week on gas, $376.00 on car insurance semiannually, and $ on oil changes quarterly. What are her total car expenses for a year?

2. She will drive a total of 10,000 miles during the year and 4,000 of them will be for business. What is Penny's deduction?

Comparing Options

In this section we explored two options for deducting your car expenses. You can either deduct your miles or deduct your actual expenses.

What Do You Think?

1. If you were Penny, which option would you choose? Why?

Deducting Meals and Entertainment

You can deduct 50% of your meals and entertainment expenses if they are work related, such as meeting with a prospective client and going to networking events.

Calculating Estimated Taxes

Your estimated taxes are based on your net income. They include two types of taxes: self-employment tax and federal income taxes.

Self-Employment Tax

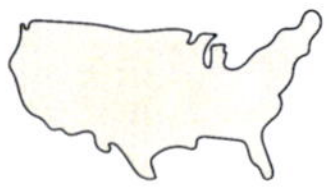

Federal Income Taxes

Self Employment Taxes

Self-employment taxes pay for Social Security and Medicare. The rates will change each year. Check www.irs.gov for more information. The rates in the book are from 2017.

Social Security
12.4%

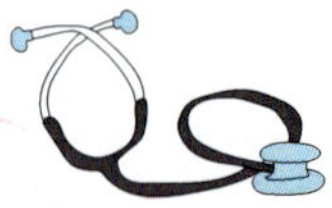

Medicare
2.9%

When You're an Employee ...

The amount you of taxes you pay for social security and Medicare are different when you work for yourself than when you work for another company. When you work for another company, your employer will pay half of them and you will pay the other half. These taxes will also be deducted from your paycheck and sent to the IRS.

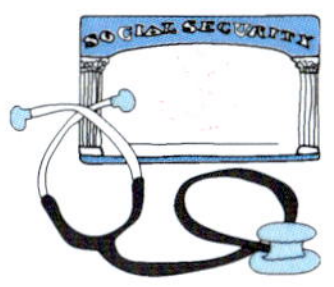

Total Social Security and Medicare

15.3% =

Employer Pays: *7.65%*

+

You Pay *7.65%*

Taxes When You're Employed

1. If Penny was an employee and earned $38,000 in taxable income, how much would she pay for social security and Medicare?

2. How much would her employer pay?

When You're Self-Employed ...

When you work for yourself, you are responsible for all of the payroll taxes. These taxes will not be automatically deducted from your paycheck, so you will need to factor them into your estimated taxes.

You pay the full amount.

15.3%

Taxes When You're a Business Owner

1. If Penny is a business owner instead whose net income is $16,905.90, how much will she pay for Social Security and Medicare?

What Do You Think?

1. Business get to subtract their business expenses before paying Social Security and Medicare taxes. Employees usually don't subtract expenses from their income. Do you think it is fair to charge business owners a higher rate for these taxes? Why or why not?

Federal Income Taxes

The other part of estimated taxes is federal income taxes. The amount you pay depends on your income.

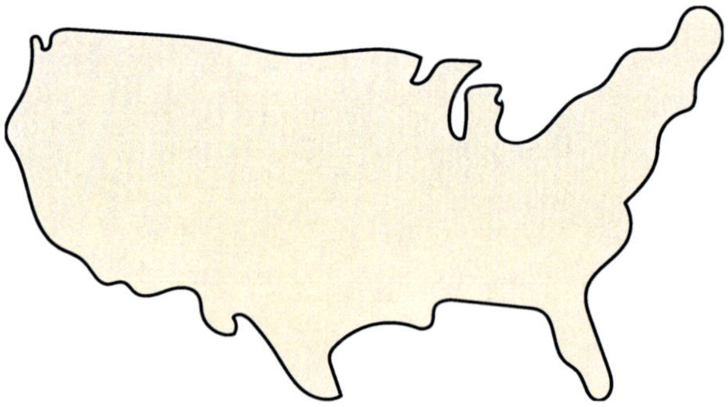

Tax Brackets

Income taxes work in brackets which means you pay a higher rate as your income increases. The rates change each year. Check with www.irs.gov for the most up-to-date rates. The rates used in this book are from 2017.

Rate	Net Income Between ...
10%	$0 - $9,325
15%	$9,325 - $37,950
25%	$37,950 - $91,900
28%	$91,900 - $191,650
33%	$191,650 - $416,700
35%	$416,700 - $418,400
39.6%	$418,400+

Penny's Bracket

1. If Penny's net income is $, which tax bracket is she in?

How Do Brackets Work?

Brackets aren't as straight forward as them seem. The money is split between the brackets. For example, if you fall into the 15% tax bracket. Part of your money will be taxed at 10% and the rest will be taxed at 15%.

Net Income
$

10% Bracket
The first $9,325 will be taxed at 10%.

15% Bracket
The rest of the money ($) will be taxed at 15%.

Penny's Income Taxes

1. If Penny's net income is $16,905.90 and she is taxed 10% for the first $9,325 and at 15% for the rest, how much tax federal income will she owe?

2. If the tax system did not split the money between the brackets and charged Penny 15% on all of her net income, how much would she owe?

Made in United States
North Haven, CT
04 November 2026

21726615R00066